Mal KS Count

SECOND EDITION

M J Bromley

au us

A member of the AUTUS GROUP LIMITED

AUTUS BOOKS
England, UK
Twitter: @AutusBooks

Making KS3 Count First Published in 2016

Second Edition First Published in 2017
This Edition © Bromley Education 2017

The right of M J Bromley to be identified as the author of this work has been asserted by him in accordance with the Copyrights, Designs and Patents Act 1988

ISBN-13: 978-1975946883

ISBN-10: 197594688X

For Henry, Maggie and Meg

Contents

Part One

Front Matter

CHAPTER ONE
Introduction to the second edition

I started writing this book in the summer of 2015 - having, over the previous decade, first as a teacher then as a school leader, become increasingly convinced that Key Stage 3 pupils were getting a rough deal from our education system. But life and work got in the way and I was forced to put the book on the back-burner. In the autumn of that year, however, Ofsted published a report called 'Key Stage 3: The Wasted Years?' which had me scrambling for my manuscript...

Ofsted's report summarised the findings of approximately 1,600 section 5 inspections carried out between September 2013 and March 2015, 318 monitoring inspections carried out between September 2014 and March 2015, 55 section 5 inspections from June and July 2015, 100 interviews with senior leaders, 10,942 questionnaire responses from pupils in Years 7, 8 and 9, and 14 good practice visits.

Rather depressingly, the report found that, while pupils generally had the opportunity to study a broad range of subjects throughout Key Stage 3, in too many schools the quality of teaching and the rate of pupils' progress and achievement were simply not good enough.

In fact, inspectors reported concerns about the effectiveness of Key Stage 3 in one in five of its routine inspections, particularly in relation to the slow progress made in English and maths and the lack of challenge for the most able pupils. Inspectors also reported significant weaknesses in modern foreign languages (MFL), history and geography at Key Stage 3.

Too often, inspectors found teaching that failed to challenge and engage pupils. Additionally, low-level disruption in some of these lessons, particularly in MFL, was deemed to have had a detrimental impact on pupils' learning.

Achievement was not good enough in just under half of the MFL classes observed, two-fifths of the history classes and one third of the geography classes.

The report claimed that the weaknesses inspectors identified in teaching and pupil progress reflected a general lack of priority given to Key Stage 3 by many secondary school leaders. For example, most leaders questioned as part of the survey admitted they staffed Key Stages 4 and 5 before Key Stage 3. Thus, too many Key Stage 3 classes were split between two or more teachers and/or were taught by non-specialists or inexperienced staff.

In this regard - and in the way schools assess and track pupils' progress - Key Stage 3 is regarded as a poor relation to other key stages.

The report also asserted that too many secondary schools did not work effectively with partner primary schools to understand pupils' prior learning and ensure that they built on this during Key Stage 3. Some secondary leaders simply accepted that pupils would needlessly repeat what they had already done in primary school during the early part of Key Stage 3, particularly in Year 7.

In addition, and this was not a feature of Key Stage 3 I'd paid particular attention to when first drafting my book in the summer, half of the pupils surveyed said that their homework never, or only some of the time, helped them to make progress. And inspectors found that, too often, homework did not consolidate or extend pupils' learning.

Finally, the report claimed that some school leaders did not use Pupil Premium funding effectively in Key Stage 3 to ensure that any differences in the outcomes of disadvantaged pupils when compared to their peers continued to be diminished following pupils' transition to secondary school. Instead, additional support tended to be focused on intervention activities at Key Stage 4, by which time they simply compensated for ineffective practice in the earlier years of secondary education.

Ofsted recommended that senior leaders should make Key Stage 3 a higher priority in all aspects of school planning, monitoring and evaluation, and ensure that not only is the curriculum offer at Key Stage 3 broad and balanced, but that teaching is of a high quality and prepares pupils for more challenging subsequent study at Key Stages 4 and 5.

Ofsted also recommended that senior leaders ensure that transition from Key Stage 2 to 3 focuses as much on pupils' academic needs as it does on their pastoral needs, and that senior leaders foster better cross-phase partnerships with primary schools to ensure that Key Stage 3 teachers build on pupils' prior knowledge, understanding and skills.

Ofsted said middle and senior leaders should make sure that systems and procedures for assessing and monitoring pupils' progress in Key Stage 3 are more robust and that leaders should focus on the needs of disadvantaged pupils in Key Stage 3, including the most able, in order to close the achievement gap as quickly as possible. Leaders should also evaluate the quality and effectiveness of homework in Key Stage 3 in order to ensure that it helps pupils to make good progress. And, finally, school leaders should put in place literacy and numeracy strategies that ensure pupils build on their prior attainment in Key Stage 2 in these crucial areas.

When I first read the report in the autumn of 2015, my immediate response was to nod along knowingly. I certainly recognised many of the challenges it outlined. For example, I knew that, when working as a deputy headteacher responsible for the school timetable, I had focused on Key Stages 4 and 5 before filling in the gaps with Key Stage 3 lessons, thus necessitating some split classes and some non-specialist teaching. I knew, too, that I'd focused a disproportionate amount of funding on intensive interventions in the dying days of GCSE, rather than using funding - and other resources - equitably across all years and key stages.

The report, therefore, articulated what I'd long known and what had spurred me to write this book in the first place. But, whilst all of Ofsted's findings were sensible, they were also - perhaps understandably for a high-level report - vague and intangible. For example, what does it mean, in reality, to give Key Stage 3 a higher priority? What, in practice, do cross-phase partnerships look like? What is robust assessment and monitoring, exactly? And what, precisely, constitutes quality and effective homework?

In short, Ofsted's report set out the challenges we face in making Key Stage 3 count, but did not proffer many solutions. And that's why I hurried back to my manuscript and finished the first edition of this book which was published in the summer of 2016.

The first edition seemed to resonate with many people working in education (and became my biggest selling book), and, thus, over the course of the last year or so, I've been invited to speak at various conferences and INSET events and have, along the way, been fortunate enough to debate the issues with hundreds, if not thousands, of wise teachers and school leaders.

Discussing the challenges of Key Stage 3 - and its possible solutions - with likeminded professionals has really helped me to develop and consolidate my thinking; what's more, I've been able to see up close which strategies work in Key Stage 3 and which do not.

This second edition is my attempt to articulate my latest thinking and to share even more practical ideas about how to improve the educational experience of pupils in Years 7, 8 and 9 in order to ensure that those three years are not wasted but are, in fact, enjoyable, challenging, and rewarding.

The secret to an effective Key Stage 3, I believe, is to:

Make transition count by ensuring that pupils are supported to transfer - not just between the different phases of education as they move from primary to secondary, but also between all the key stages and years of compulsory schooling as pupils transfer between Years 7, 8 and 9 - gradually and smoothly;

Make the curriculum count by ensuring that there is a greater sense of continuity between primary and secondary schools both in terms of what is taught and when it is taught, and by ensuring that the way in which the curriculum is taught is challenging, engaging and different to that which precedes and succeeds it, and provides for the effective development of literacy and numeracy skills;

Make homework count by ensuring that homework enables pupils to practice their prior learning, provides a real audience, purpose and context, and is an optimum volume to support and yet not demotivate pupils;

Make data count by improving the quality and effectiveness of target-setting, assessment, and tracking in order to ensure that the regular monitoring of progress leads to frequent, formative feedback, and timely interventions and support which seek to diminish any differences in the performance of different groups of pupils.

As such, the 'meat' of this book, sandwiched between its front and end matter, is divided into four distinct parts focusing on:

1. Making transition count
2. Making the curriculum count
3. Making homework count
4. Making data count

CHAPTER TWO
The cannibalisation of Key Stage 3

The 2015 'Wasted Years' report I summarised in the previous chapter was published during Sir Michael Wilshaw's tenure as Her Majesty's Chief Inspector of Schools. In December 2016, however, he regenerated into Amanda Spielman (albeit without shafts of yellow light thrusting from every limb, the trademark of transition for the new Doctor Who).

After a quiet start in post, Spielman gave a speech at the Festival of Education in June 2017 which got the education world talking. In that speech, Spielman trumpeted the importance of the school curriculum.

She said that, all too often, schools lose sight of the real substance of education: "Not the exam grades or the progress scores, important though they are, but instead the real meat of what is taught in our schools and colleges: the curriculum."

She said that, although it's true that education should prepare young people to succeed in life and make their contribution in the labour market, "to reduce education down to this kind of functionalist level is rather wretched."

Education, she argued, "should be about broadening minds, enriching communities and advancing civilisation" and "ultimately, it is about leaving the world a better place than we found it."

She said that this reductionist, functionalist attitude was evident in the way schools tracked GCSE assessment objectives all the way back to Year 7, and started SAT practice papers as early as Year 4. She said this attitude was also evident - and this is the crux of the matter for us - in the increasing "cannibalisation of key stage 3 into key stage 4".

"Preparing for GCSEs so early," Spielman said, "gives young people less time to study a range of subjects in depth and more time just practising the tests themselves."

We have, she said, "a full and coherent national curriculum and [it is] a huge waste not to use it properly."

Indeed, all children should study a broad and rich curriculum and yet "curtailing key stage 3 means prematurely cutting this off for children who may never have an opportunity to study some of these subjects again."

Spielman said "scrapping most of your curriculum through Year 6 to focus just on English and maths" is equally misguided and does "pupils a disservice".

In short, Spielman said that all the above practices reflect "a tendency to mistake badges and stickers for learning itself... [and put] the interests of schools ahead of the interests of the children in them."

"We should be ashamed," she said, "that we have let such behaviour persist for so long."

Of course, it's not difficult to see why such behaviour has persisted for so long: the government's accountability system, centred on performance tables, is undoubtedly at the heart of the matter, aided and abetted by Ofsted itself who's starting point for inspection is the previous year's outcomes and the current year's predicted outturn.

Stakes are high and schools must ensure that Key Stage 2 SAT and GCSE outcomes are above the floor standard and that the line drawn between the two sets of tests represents good progress for pupils. What's more, with a school's reputation and future at risk, not to mention jobs, it's unsurprising that so many schools have attempted to game the system in any which way they can.

But the sorts of 'system-gaming' Spielman bemoans - narrowing the Key Stage 2 curriculum to English and maths, starting GCSE study in Year 9 and tracking GCSE objectives from Year 7 onwards - are clearly not in pupils' best interests. These behaviours put league table performance ahead of what's morally right for young people, and thus stand opposed to what is understood by a good education.

But, as she says, these behaviours have persisted for a long time so surely now is the time for change?

I, for one, am pleased that the Chief Inspector has highlighted these issues and, as a result, given them the column inches they deserve, because they add further weight to the arguments in this book.

As I say above, it's not difficult to understand why school leaders prioritise Key Stages 4 and 5 over Key Stage 3 because this is where external accountability sits and it takes a brave, perhaps foolish, headteacher to focus on Key Stage 3 at the possible expense of - in the short-term at least - GCSE and A Level outcomes. But putting all your eggs in one GCSE basket - including starting Key Stage 4 in Year 9 and using GCSE assessment criteria from Year 7 - is clearly short-sighted and makes a mockery of Key Stage 3.

Key Stage 3 must not be regarded as a poor relation to Key Stage 4 for this will only prove to be a vicious cycle.

In practice, this means that school leaders - particularly the timetabler - need to avoid the temptation to schedule Key Stages 4 and 5 first then fill in the gaps with Key Stage 3 lessons, thus increasing the chances of Key Stage 3 classes being split between two or more teachers.

It also means avoiding timetabling non-specialist, underperforming and/or inexperienced teachers for Key Stage 3 lessons. School leaders should utilise their best teachers because this will pay dividends in later years and limit the need of remedial interventions to help pupils catch up for lost time.

In addition to being appropriately staffed, the Key Stage 3 curriculum should strike the right balance between providing pupils with a grounding for GCSE and being different enough to Key Stage 4 to be engaging.

As well as providing a springboard for GCSE, Key Stage 3 needs to flow naturally from Key Stage 2...

The Wasted Years report, as we have already seen, said that too many secondary schools do not work effectively with partner primary schools in order to understand pupils' prior learning and therefore ensure that they build on this during Key Stage 3. Indeed, some secondary leaders simply accept that pupils will repeat what they had already done in primary school during the early part of Key Stage 3.

This problem, sadly, has only worsened since the government implemented its new national curricula...

Richard Hudson, emeritus professor of linguistics at University College, London, who was part of an expert group advising the government on the primary curriculum, has since admitted that the process - overseen by the then Education Secretary, Michael Gove - was "chaotic".

Hudson says that, as a result, the new curriculum and assessments are not based on good research evidence and, as such, many primary teachers are not equipped to teach it.

Hudson is not alone in criticising the new primary curriculum he helped to write. Indeed, all four members of the expert panel have spoken publicly about their concerns.

The government's key curriculum adviser, Tim Oates, has also warned that the spelling, punctuation and grammar (SPaG) tests "need a rethink [because there is a] genuine problem about [the] undue complexity of demand [of the] "language about language" that pupils are now expected to know.

David Crystal, one of Britain's leading English language experts, has argued that the SPaG test, and its underlying view of language, "turns the clock back half a century" because it places too much emphasis on simply spotting and labelling linguistic features and regards this as an end in itself rather than as a starting point that enables discussions about effective writing. In other words, grammatical features are now taught out of context and without purpose, and yet just because a pupil can recognise a split digraph or a fronted adverbial doesn't mean they can write any better.

Hudson, in an interview with the Guardian in May 2017, recalled the disorganised process of writing the curriculum:

"To give you an idea of how chaotic things were, when [the expert panel] was originally put together, we had about four meetings and were supposed to be devising a grammar curriculum to cover the whole of compulsory education: primary and secondary. We started off with the primary curriculum, which we were a bit unconfident about as none of us had much experience of primary education and were looking forward to getting stuck into the real thing: secondary.

"Then the DfE pulled the plug by saying: 'We are not going to do any secondary curriculum.' So [the primary curriculum that] was published was meant to be about building the foundations for the real thing. But that's all there is."

There is so much with which to take issue in what Hudson says. Firstly, the fact the primary curriculum was written by a panel without primary teaching experience is somewhat troubling and goes a little way to explain why the result is so disappointing. It might also help explain why children were left in tears when they sat the first reading test in 2016 because it required a reading age of fourteen.

Also, to suggest that the secondary curriculum was "the real thing" is deeply insulting to primary colleagues and fundamentally wrongheaded.

And, finally, the fact that the panel's plans to develop a secondary curriculum that flowed from the primary one were abandoned explains why there is such a disconnect between the two and why pupils experience such difficulty following transition.

Hudson went on to say that the result is "terribly worrying, because it means that all the work children do in primary is wasted, as they probably won't take it on in secondary."

As I say above, the government did produce a new secondary curriculum in English, but it was a slimmed down, less prescriptive version of what had gone before, and therefore did not build upon the foundations laid down by the primary curriculum.

The emphasis on grammatical terminology has also been criticised by academics because there is no research evidence to suggest that this approach helps improve children's writing. Indeed, when asked whether there was any evidence at the time that a greater emphasis on traditional grammar was developmentally appropriate for children, Hudson said: "No, there was no evidence, and we were guessing. But I think we were right."

Another member of that four-strong panel, Debra Myhill - director of the centre for research in writing at the University of Exeter - has said she wants the SPaG tests scrapped.

In a submission to parliament, she said that the tests should be discontinued "because they serve no valid educational purpose". She added that the way the tests are designed is flawed and that "children are developing grammatical misconceptions ... caused by an over-emphasis on naming and identifying [technical terms simply] for test purposes".

"There is no evidence," Myhill said, "that being able to name and identify linguistic terminology has any effect on your use of language."

So, in short, we have a new primary curriculum that is much more prescriptive than that which preceded it. However, because it proved so problematic to write and implement, the government abandoned its plan to follow it with a progressive secondary curriculum. The secondary curriculum the government did eventually introduce was less prescriptive. Thus, the primary curriculum does not flow naturally into the secondary curriculum and the knowledge and skills taught at Key Stage 3 do not build upon that which is taught in Key Stage 2.

This disconnect, as we have seen, is particularly true in English where pupils now finish Year 6 with an impressively detailed knowledge of grammatical terms (albeit taught out of context rather than through the teaching of great texts), but most secondary teachers don't know what has been taught and do not have the same level of subject knowledge as their pupils.

If I did not have a primary aged daughter, for example, I would not know what a 'split digraph' was and yet I've been teaching English for 15 years! Nor would I know that primary pupils are now taught about 'conjunctions' rather than 'connectives'. (One quick fix for this is for every Year 7 teacher to download and read the glossary of grammatical terms taught in the primary curriculum.)

The problem seems to be that curriculum reforms have been implemented in isolation, and primary and secondary schools don't have enough time to talk to each other about what and how they teach. What's more, the government hasn't provided - or equipped schools with the funding for - staff training on the new curriculum and so many teachers are working in the dark.

Another consequence of this lack of joined up thinking on the curriculum is that the primary curriculum now better prepares pupils for the new, more demanding GCSEs but renders pointless the three years of Key Stage 3 sandwiched in between.

This poses an additional challenge to secondary schools than those already outlined in The Wasted Years report: what can we do in Years 7, 8 and 9 to ensure that pupils are challenged, engaged and making progress? One answer, I think, in English at least, is to put into context the technical terminology now taught at primary. This involves reading and writing increasingly complex texts, developing a love of reading for reading's sake, and developing pupils' ability to write in a range of contexts, for a variety of purposes, and in different styles.

Another solution is to ensure that pupils are fed a rich diet of subjects from across the arts, humanities, languages and sciences, and are afforded experiences outside the classroom by visiting museums and art galleries, theatres and monuments. In short, schools should do as Spielman advises and ensure that the Key Stage 3 curriculum broadens minds, enriches communities, and advances civilisation. That way, Key Stage 3 will leave the world a better place than pupils found it...and no one could claim that the years spent doing that were wasted.

Part Two

Making Transition Count

CHAPTER THREE
Primary to secondary transition

Why do we need to improve transition?

Why do we need to improve the process of transition from primary to secondary school as pupils move from Year 6 into 7?

Well, per Galton (1999), almost forty per cent of children fail to make expected progress during the year immediately following a change of schools and DfE data from 2011 shows that average progress drops between Key Stage 2 and Key Stage 3 for reading, writing and maths. Moreover, the effects of transition are amplified by risk factors such as poverty and ethnicity.

And why should this be? Primarily, I believe, it's because there is insufficient or ineffective communication between primary and secondary schools and this has several harmful consequences...

Firstly, secondary school teachers have a weak understanding of the curriculum content that precedes what they personally teach whilst primary school teachers have a weak understanding of the curriculum that succeeds their own. In practice, this means that the curriculum is not joined up and that pupils are taught content and skills more than once or are taught the same concepts in contradictory ways.

Secondly, assessment practices in the two phases are inconsistent and therefore there is little correlation between Year 6 and 7 data. This leads to a lack of trust on both sides of the 'divide' in terms of the validity of assessment data and to pupils being re-tested at the start of Year 7 just weeks after sitting stressful, high stakes Key Stage 2 SATs. It also generates confusion and even animosity amongst parents who perceive that their sons and daughters are regressing when in fact the data may mask their progress or, at any rate, exaggerate the decline.

Thirdly, and in part a further consequence of the first two points above but also the result of pedagogical differences between the two phases, there is often a weak understanding in Year 7 of what pupils can achieve and therefore insufficient challenge in the curriculum.

How can we improve transition?

There are five broad categories of school life - sometimes referred to as 'bridges' - in which the transition process can be improved:

1. Administrative
2. Social and personal
3. Curricular
4. Pedagogic
5. Managing learning

The administrative 'bridge' is concerned with the general management of the transition process such as the formal liaison between a secondary school and its feeder primaries, usually at a senior leadership level. In practice, this might take the form of the transfer of pupil records and achievement data, meetings with pupils and parents, and visits from headteachers, senior leaders and teachers.

The social and personal 'bridge' is concerned with forging links between pupils/parents and their new school prior to and immediately after transfer. It is also concerned with the pupil induction process into their new school and might take the form of induction days, open evenings, school orientation activities, team-building days, taster classes, the production and issuing of prospectuses and booklets, and so on.

The curricular 'bridge' is concerned with improving curriculum continuity between the primary and secondary phases of education by sharing plans that show what content is taught on either side of the transition. This involves teachers rather than senior leaders and might take the form of cross-phase teaching, the teaching of bridging units at the end of Year 6 and start of Year 7, summer schools, joint CPD networks and INSET days, the sharing of good practice and shared planning, and teacher exchanges.

Whereas the curricular bridge is concerned with *what* pupils are taught, the pedagogic 'bridge' is concerned with establishing a shared understanding of *how* pupils are taught - as well as how they learn - in order to achieve a greater continuity in classroom practice and teaching. This is achieved by understanding differing teaching styles and skills, by engaging in shared CPD and teacher exchanges, and by primary and secondary teachers observing each other in practice.

The managing learning 'bridge' is about ensuring that pupils are active participants, rather than passive observers, in the transition process. This is achieved by empowering pupils and their parents with information about achievement and empowering them with the confidence to articulate their learning needs in a new environment. This might take the form of giving information to parents/pupils, providing pupils with learning portfolios and samples of achievements, and raising pupils' awareness of their needs and talents by sharing and explaining data.

What would an effective transition look like?

There are, I believe, three main measures of an effective transition process:

1. Social adjustment
2. Institutional adjustment
3. Curriculum interest and continuity

Social adjustment is about pupils successfully making new friends and reporting higher self-esteem.

Institutional adjustment is about pupils settling in well at their new school and getting used to their new school's routines, systems and structures.

Curriculum interest and continuity is about pupils being prepared for the level and style of work they encounter at secondary school, as well as being appropriately challenged and engaged, and building on the progress they made at primary school.

Putting it into practice...

So, we need to span the river that flows between primary and secondary schools with five transition 'bridges' so that we can safely reach our destination: the shores of social adjustment, institutional adjustment, and curriculum interest and continuity.

But what does this look like in practice? What do we need to do in order to improve our transition arrangements? Here are some suggested actions...

We can arrange **regular visits from secondary school teachers** to Year 6 to talk about life in 'big school' and, perhaps an even more impactful strategy, we can arrange for regular visits from Year 7 pupils to talk to Year 6 and share their experiences of the transition process and of life after transition. Pupils are more likely to listen to their peers than they are to their teachers and will be relieved to hear from pupils in the year above them that life in 'big school' isn't quite as daunting as they think.

Feeder primary schools can operate an **open-door policy for parents** to air any concerns and questions. Secondary schools, meanwhile, can hold a parents' evening in the summer term to welcome new parents and answer questions about the transition and induction process, and a further parents' evening in the autumn term for 'settling in' discussions and to talk to their child's form tutor.

We can make sure that all **staff have clear roles and responsibilities** that make explicit the part they play in securing a smooth and successful transition for pupils.

We can make sure each year and each department has a '**transition expert**' who is afforded the time (and possibly remunerated) to become the go-to person for all aspects of transition. For example, a transition expert within the English department of a secondary school could make it their mission to know as much as possible about the primary English curriculum and could map what is taught at primary, including the glossary of grammatical terms pupils must know by the end of Year 6, to the Key Stage 3 curriculum. They could ensure that what is taught in Year 7 represents a natural progression from what is taught in Year 6, and that it consolidates and extends prior learning. They could also ensure that the language of learning used in Years 6 and 7 is consistent - both in terms of the technical language pupils know and use (for example, using the word 'conjunction' rather than 'connective' to describe 'and'), and the language teachers use to describe aspects of pedagogy and practice (for example, WAGOLL and WABOLL). This expert could be the main liaison with primary feeder schools, too. They might, for example, work with primary colleagues on developing a bridging unit and on teaching a summer school.

As well as recruiting transition experts in each year and/or department, we can make sure that every teacher in each phase and stage develops a **deeper knowledge of the curriculum content** and means of assessment from the preceding and succeeding phases and stages to that which they teach. This means Year 6 teachers reading the secondary curriculum and familiarising themselves with the way in which their pupils will be assessed when they move into Year 7 (which, with 'assessment without levels' may be different in each of the secondary schools to which pupils transfer). It also means those Year 6 teachers speaking to and observing Year 7 teachers to understand how the curriculum is taught and what is expected of pupils. Likewise, it means Year 7 teachers reading the primary curriculum and familiarising themselves with the KS2 SATs and other forms of teacher assessment in Year 6. It means talking to and observing Year 6 teachers. Of course, observing teaching in the phase before or after that which you teach is time-consuming and may require lessons to be covered. But, in my view, it is one of the most impactful forms of CPD in which a teacher can engage and time and money well-spent. What's more, I would recommend senior leaders provide class cover to enable their teachers to visit and observe other teachers. Not only are school leaders often better placed to cover lessons because they know the pupils and are less likely to encounter behavioural problems, teaching cover lessons is a great way to 'lead by example' as well as - for those leaders without timetabled lessons - 'keep their hand in' and feel the impact of the decisions they make in the classroom.

We can run **joint social events** between Year 6 and Year 7, such as a disco in the summer term. This would more naturally take place in the secondary school to enable Year 6 pupils to experience secondary school life and become familiar with the buildings.

We can ensure that **transition days**, whereby Year 6s visit their new school in the summer term prior to transfer, strike the right balance between enthusing pupils about what delights await them in September (and allaying their fears) AND not over-selling the secondary experience. We want the day to be fun and engaging, to make pupils excited about starting their new school, but we don't want to give the false impression that every science lesson, say, is a veritable firework display or that every day is full of fun, because the reality will only prove disappointing by contrast and pupils will feel cheated.

We can ask Year 6 pupils to produce a **Pupil Passport** or portfolio which contains examples of their best work and information about how they like to learn and about what motivates them. This puts some ownership of the transition process into pupils' hands, thus engaging them as active participants in the process rather just passive recipients whereby transition is done to them by others.

Year 6 teachers need to **help pupils become increasingly 'secondary ready'** as they travel towards transition. For example, they need to help pupils to understand their strengths and areas for improvement, and to develop their ability to talk confidently to their teachers. This necessitates primary teachers observing and working with their secondary colleagues to understand what a secondary classroom looks and sounds like, then starting to emulate it. Of course, this is a two-way process and secondary teachers also need to observe and work with their primary colleagues to ensure the beginning of Year 7 more closely resembles the end of primary school and slowly bridges the gap between primary and secondary ways of working. In short, both sides of the divide need to adjust in order to ensure pupils are eased through transition.

Another strategy to help bridge the gap between the primary and secondary curriculum is to use a **mixed model of curriculum delivery in Year** 7. For example, there might be some project-based learning whereby several subject areas (say, all the humanities, all the sciences, all the arts) combine to create one cross-curricular project. This not only helps pupils to see the natural links between subjects (and helps improve their ability to 'transfer' knowledge and skills from one context to another), it also helps to reduce the number of different teachers and subjects to which a new Year 7 pupil - used to working with one or two teachers all year in primary school) will be exposed. As well as project-based learning, pupils in Year 7 may have some subjects taught by their form tutor in their form room. Again, this helps limit the number of teachers and classrooms - and therefore the logistical transition along busy corridors - pupils have to encounter and it helps foster a sense of belonging and emotional stability. The Year 7 timetable can also be blocked creatively - for example, in a two-week timetable by mirroring weeks 1 and 2 so pupils have less information to remember, and by scheduling double lessons - to reduce the number of transitions pupils must make and to facilitate the creation of nurture groups for the most vulnerable pupils.

We can have a **staggered start** to the new academic year so that new Year 7 pupils can acclimatise to their new environment and navigate around the site without the looming presence of older, bigger students. This might extend into staggered breaks and lunches for the first week so that new Year 7 pupils can experience lunch in the canteen without vying for position with older pupils and can enjoy the play grounds, and make new friends, without fear.

We can make sure that transition arrangements are not confined to the transfer of pupils from Year 6 into Year 7 but also cover the other transitions that pupils encounter. In other words, transition should not just be about pupils' transfer from one phase of compulsory schooling to another, but also about the transition pupils experience between the key stages and years of school life. For example, we can put in place transition arrangements to **support pupils as they move from Year 7 into Year 8, from Year 8 and into Year 9, and from key stage 3 into key stage 4**, bridging the gap between KS3 and GCSE study. At each stage, transition arrangements should be put in place for pupils but also their parents/carers.

We can get pupils to **start a new book or folder in the final half-term of every year** which they will take with them into the next year. Not only does this focus their attentions on producing their best work, it provides the next teacher with ready examples of what pupils can achieve when outside of test conditions and in their comfort zones. This simple act can aid target-setting and lesson planning - pitching work in pupils' 'struggle zones' - better than end of year tests.

Another strategy to help pupils transition from one year to the next is to **start the new timetable before the summer**. Often, once Year 11 pupils have concluded their studies, there is flexibility to start the next year's timetable so that pupils and teachers get to know each other in the final few weeks of term. This enables teachers to set the tone and make clear their expectations, and affords the opportunity to set homework to be completed over the summer holiday, better preparing pupils for the start of September. If this wholesale adoption of the new timetable is not logistically possible, then the same goals can be achieved on a smaller scale by pupils attending 'taster classes' with their new teachers once or twice in the last couple of weeks and by work being set for the summer holidays.

Another means of improving the transfer of pupils at every stage of their education - not just from primary to secondary school - is to establish **peer mentoring** schemes. Although research recommends that a reading mentor be at least two years older (and have a reading age at least two years greater) than the mentee, there is much to be said for enlisting Year 8 pupils as mentors for new Year 7s. Year 8s have more recently experienced transition and settling in arrangements, and thus are better placed to offer relevant advice and guidance. Being closer in age and experience, they are also better placed to communicate and understand how a Year 7 pupil is feeling. What's more, Year 8 - as I will explain later - is often regarded as the most wasted of the so-called 'wasted years', sandwiched between the exciting newness of Year 7 and the more meaningful curriculum of Year 9 with its elective subjects and end-of-key stage tests. As such, Year 8 pupils would likely benefit from being given leadership opportunities, and a sense of responsibility and purpose. The mentoring could start whilst the mentees are in Year 6 and the mentors in Year 7 (on transition days, for example) and continue after the summer of transfer.

We can ensure we secure more and earlier parental engagement including via telephone calls, emails, texts, and face-to-face visits. As well as engaging the parents of current Year 6 pupils before and during transition, we could make good use of their experiences after transition has concluded. For example, we could elicit parental feedback on their - and their child's - experience of the transition process, finding out what worked and what did not. Indeed, schools in both phases need to evaluate and adapt their transition plans to take account of **pupil, parent and teacher feedback**. And, to do this, both primary and secondary schools need to collect feedback at every available opportunity.

I will explore cross phase projects more fully later but suffice to say there is much to be gained by **Year 6 and Year 7 teachers working collaboratively on their curriculum planning**. This is no more important than in the final half-term of Year 6 and the first half-term of Year 7 where curriculum content and pedagogy need to meld. In so doing, Year 6 and 7 teachers can establish a shared language of learning and establish common processes for, for example, how they run self- and peer-assessment and group work. Cross-phase partnerships might include joint primary and secondary CPD events and INSET days and peer observation schemes.

Another useful product of this cross-phase partnership working is to create a '**bridging unit**' which pupils begin working on at the end of Year 6 (perhaps after they have sat their SATs), continue working on over the summer holidays and complete at the start of Year 7. Bridging units enable pupils to produce good work to take with them to secondary school which shows their new teachers what they're capable of achieving. They also allay some of pupils' natural apprehensions about the kind of work they'll be expected to do in secondary school. And bridging units help pupils to see the natural links between the primary and secondary curricula, and to understand that secondary education is about progression not about starting again.

Of course, extra consideration will be needed for those pupils who do not have supportive homes and who will therefore be placed at a disadvantage when continuing their work over the summer holidays. To resolve this, it may be advisable to **run a 'summer school'** which enables pupils to access help and support in school. Although discrete summer schools funding has been scrapped, it is a good use of Pupil Premium funding and the literacy and numeracy catch-up funding.

Another consideration to take if running bridging units is whether, as a secondary school, you have access to and support from every feeder primary school. If not, working with some pupils but not all could lead to an attainment gap. If you do not have access to all feeders, it doesn't mean the strategy should be abandoned, however. Bridging units are hugely beneficial, after all. Rather, it means taking mitigating action to support those pupils who study at primary schools with whom you cannot liaise. For example, pupils who are not going to start the unit in Year 6 lessons could do some of the work at home or after-hours at the secondary school.

Cloud services and other technological means of communicating and sharing information can also be used to engage the parents of pupils in primary schools with which there is little contact or collaboration (as well as hard-to-reach parents). For example, it may be possible to send the Year 6 unit and any work that's required over the summer break directly to parents using Google Drive or OneDrive. Work can also be submitted by parents or pupils in this way, ensuring no one is unduly disadvantaged by being in a primary school which, for whatever reason, does not engage in the teaching of bridging units.

Whilst we're on the subject of cross-phase working, another useful strategy for primary and secondary teachers to employ when working together to improve transition, is to **map the curriculum content covered - and the skills required of pupils - in Years 6 and** 7, and then to audit which skills are explicitly taught and when, thus identifying any gaps whereby pupils are expected to know or be able to do something which they haven't been taught. These gaps then need to be filled so the process comes full circle as teachers plan where to teach these skills. Of course, once a skill has been taught for the first time, say in Year 6, we need to decide if it needs to be re-taught again when it is needed next (and, if so, whether we need to completely re-teach it or just recap and practice).

What might all this look like to pupils?

Let's look at an imaginary transition process starting in Year 5, working through to Year 7...

Year 5

Transition should not begin in the summer term of Year 6. It needs to begin much earlier in order to effective. In Year 5, for example, there might be specialist visits and workshops led by secondary teachers from various curriculum areas. These not only provide pupils with a flavour of the subject specialisms and teacher expertise they would otherwise be denied but also enable pupils to familiarise themselves with their future teachers and their teaching styles.

Also in Year 5, the headteacher of the secondary school might provide a tour of their school during the day to provide pupils with the experience of 'big school' and allay some of the fears that inevitably fester as the rumour mill begins to grind. Other senior leaders, particularly the leader responsible for transition and the SENCO, might pay regular visits to primary schools to talk to pupils and meet with parents. And there might be ongoing close liaison between Year 5 and Year 6 teachers within the primary school in order to identify children who might potentially experience issues around transition. The school might then identify key opportunities within the Year 6 curriculum to support the development of the requisite skills these vulnerable pupils will need to survive and thrive in secondary school.

Year 6

Autumn Term
In the autumn term of Year 6, there might be forums in which the transition programme is shared with pupils and there is an opportunity to answer pupils' questions. This might be followed by open days and information evenings at secondary school for prospective pupils and their parents. Parents may also request additional meetings with leaders and teachers from the secondary school such as the SENCO. Also in the autumn term, parents will complete an on-line application form for the secondary schools of their choice so primary schools might need to provide support during this process.

Spring Term
In the spring term of Year 6, secondary schools will receive a list of admissions and parents will receive confirmation of their child's place. Transfer forms will be sent to feeder primary schools to gather information on all pupils. Primary schools will need to gather permission from their Year 6 pupils to attach one-page profiles to their transfer forms. Primary and secondary

staff might then liaise in order to discuss pupils' strengths, interests and possible support needs.

Secondary staff might also visit their primary feeder schools to talk with Year 6 pupils about their proposed transition programme and to receive information from pupils, parents and staff, as well as offer opportunities for discussion. Year 7 pupils might visit primary schools to speak to Year 6 about their recent experience of transition and answer questions in order to allay any fears. At this stage, staff might identify vulnerable pupils and put in place a raft of additional support with the transition process, including, perhaps, a dedicated teaching assistant for transition.

A letter might be sent to parents/carers to inform them of their child's inclusion in specialist transition work. Small groups of vulnerable pupils might begin meeting their transition worker on a regular basis.

Summer Term
In the summer term of Year 6, there might be a pupil and parent/carer consultation on transition procedures and a further open evening to provide parents with an opportunity to meet key staff such as their child's head of year, form tutor, SENCO, the school nurse, the school's caterers, the head boy and head girl, and so on. Parents might also be invited to make fifteen minute appointments with their child's form tutor for June/July and use the opportunity to visit their child's new classroom. The summer term might also provide opportunities for parents to purchase new uniform.

Also in the summer term, the secondary school SENCO and possibly an EAL teacher might provide summaries on high needs children in the Year 6 cohort for their secondary colleagues alongside the one-page profiles which include information on 'how best to support me' written by the child. The one-page profiles might then be reviewed and updated by pupils and their teachers.

There might also be Year 6 pupil transfer days in which pupils visit their secondary schools and take part in sample lessons, experience the lunchtime routine and take part in an orientation activity to get to know their way around the school building and grounds.

Curriculum areas might begin planning transition projects to be taught in the autumn term. A letter of introduction might be written by the headteacher or senior leader responsible for transition and sent to all Year 6 pupils. A tutor meeting with parents and pupils might take place in which the home-school agreement is discussed and signed. And a prospectus and transition booklet might be given to the pupils.

Year 7

In the autumn term of Year 7, the secondary school will welcome new pupils and this might involve a staggered start to the year in which only Year 7 are present on the first day and in which breaks and lunches are staggered for the first week to allow new pupils some space and freedom to become familiar and comfortable with the buildings and routines. There might also be an alternative timetable for the first week and a series of transition activities such as team-building events or cross-curricular projects to develop key skills. There might also be a parents' evening in order to outline the transition arrangements and afford parents the opportunity to meet their child's form tutor and head of year, as well as to familiarise themselves with the new school.

CHAPTER FOUR
Transition days

Two schools, both alike in dignity, in fair academia, where we lay our scene...

Imagine you've taught in the same school since you qualified. Now, after many happy years, you're on the move. You've secured a promotion in the school down the road and start in September. You've already met your new boss a couple of times and have read the school prospectus and staff handbook cover-to-cover, over and over. Now, your new headteacher has invited you in to her school for a day before the summer holidays to help you acclimatise.

What would you need to have accomplished by the end of the day in order to consider your visit a success, do you think? What would help you make the move?

Of course, it's not all about you! A workplace visit is a two-way process. There are some things your new school will need you to do – such as have your photo taken for your staff badge and read and sign the school's IT policy before setting you up on the school network. And there are some things you will need to do in order to better prepare yourself and alleviate some of your natural anxieties – such as familiarising yourself with the school's expectations of lesson planning, getting to grips with their assessment policy, and feeling the shape of the school day.

Imagine how you're feeling on the morning of your visit. Excited? Almost certainly. It's a new job and a promotion at that. You can't wait to get started. A little apprehensive, perhaps? It's a big change, there will be lots of new systems and structures to get used to. You've only known the inner workings of one school before. It will be a steep learning curve, that's for sure.

Now imagine how you'd feel if, upon arrival, rather than a coffee in the staff room and a friendly chat with the head, you are shepherded into a windowless room and made to sit several exams.

It would feel soul-destroying, wouldn't it? You'd feel under intense pressure, determined to do well and make a good first impression, but nervous about what would happen if you failed the tests – would it mean you'd lose the job before you'd even started it? Whatever the consequences, you'd certainly be embarrassed if the results were not good.

And what does this testing regime say about your new school? Is that what it's going to be like in your new job? No tea and comfort, no supportive chats, no arm round the shoulders and reassurance?

Whatever your anxiety, imagine how much worse it would be if you were only eleven years old and therefore less socially and emotionally developed, less used to life changes.

Now think about what your school does on its transition day in July.

Many schools do exactly what I've described above: they use the opportunity to test pupils in English and maths in order to get baseline data for setting classes and writing targets. Personally, I feel this is misguided and potentially harmful.

Other schools, in contrast, strap their pupils into a rollercoaster and give their new pupils an exciting, high octane ride through the very best that secondary school has to offer. Every 'taster' lesson is a veritable firework display – literally in the case of science. Teachers are funny and self-effacing, relaxed and patient, and lessons are fun-packed and short, punctuated by lots of 'down time' to socialise. I feel this is – though perhaps not quite as misguided as testing pupils – potentially harmful, too, because it proffers a false promise upon which reality inevitably fails to deliver.

My advice? Ensure your transition days strike the right balance between enthusing pupils about what delights await them in September (whilst also allaying their fears) and giving them a realistic vision of the future.

In short, don't test and don't over-sell the secondary experience.

You want the day to be fun and engaging, to make pupils excited about starting their new school, but you don't want to give the false impression that every day is full of fun and social time, because the reality will not only prove disappointing by contrast but pupils will also feel mis-sold and cheated. This may then demotivate them in September.

What you should avoid on transition days – which often fall hot on the heels of high-stakes, high-pressure key stage 2 SATs – is testing…

Some schools understandably want to re-test pupils to help determine which sets they will be in. Personally, I would argue that, in an ideal world where SATs results and Year 6 teacher assessments are trusted and where primary and secondary colleagues work more collaboratively, re-testing should not be necessary. After all, what message does it send to pupils if they are re-tested prior to or immediately after starting Year 7? That their SATs were pointless? That everything they've achieved to date was for nothing? And to what extent does further testing punish pupils and pile on more emotional pressure?

No, I don't much like re-testing. But…. I understand and accept that some schools feel re-testing is necessary and therefore use CATs tests or other diagnostics assessments. So, re-test if you feel you must but please don't do it on a transition day.

I happen to agree that the best time to do it is not at the start of September immediately following transfer – it's not the best start for pupils who are already feeling nervous, discomforted and unconfident. And September is too late if the test results are to be used to inform setting and targets. Tests should, therefore, be carried out before the summer when pupils are more confident and comfortable – the big fishes in the little pond – and when the results of the tests can be used to set pupils from the start of September and help with target-setting, rather than after pupils have been organised into sets and may then need to be moved up or down.

However, the July transition day is not – in my view – the time or the place for this. Transition days are precious, you should value them and use them wisely to help your new pupils adjust to secondary life and to make friends. You should use transition days to help pupils grow in confidence and self-esteem, and become accustomed to the systems and structures they'll have to work within from September.

If you really want to know what to do on these days, then ask your current Year 7s and their parents. What would have helped them make the move more smoothly? What did they enjoy about their transition day last year and what, conversely, made them feel more anxious?

CHAPTER FIVE
Transition for pupils with SEND

Our school years are amongst the most emotionally and mentally challenging because - whilst we're at school, more than at any other time in our lives - we experience myriad transitions: there are changes to our teachers and teaching assistants; changes to the year groups, classes, and schools we attend; changes to the culture and learning environment in which we study (as we move from nursery to primary school, from primary school to secondary, and from secondary school to further or higher education); changes to the level of difficulty offered by the ever-evolving curriculum; changes to the nature and level of expectations that are placed upon us; changes to the resources and support available to us; and changes to our home lives, too.

And this lengthy list ignores the fact that our bodies begin to change, too, as we transition through puberty.

How we respond to all these transitions can determine whether we succeed or fail, and influence the extent to which we develop resilience, patience, self-efficacy, and other social skills that are required later in life.

The emotional and mental effects of all these changes are amplified for pupils with special educational needs and disabilities (SEND). Accordingly, one of the SENCo's main duties is to help pupils with SEND manage these transitions and reduce the negative impact they can have on pupils' education and wellbeing.

So far in this book we've talked about improving transition in general terms. The question remains, however, how can we improve transition for pupils with SEND?

Firstly, collaboration between primary and secondary schools needs to take place both before and after pupils with SEND transfer from primary school...

The Department for Education conducted research in 2008 across seven local authorities involving forty-seven primary and secondary schools (including some special schools) in order to explore what could strengthen their transfer and transition practices. Their report concluded that effective transfer did not involve one key stage 'doing' transfer to the next, but an equal partnership that had professionally developed all stakeholders.

Galton et al. (1999, 2003) also highlighted the importance of Year 6 and Year 7 teachers working together to plan and teach 'bridging units' (projects which were started towards the end of Year 6 and completed at the start of Year 7) to help inform and personalise the pupil transfer experience.

Other examples of effective collaboration might include planning schemes of work that promote curriculum continuity and a consistency of teaching and learning styles. It might include the facilitation and support of local cross-phase networking meetings of families of schools to jointly plan for strengthening transfer and the joint working between teachers in different key stages to promote an understanding of pupils' abilities and levels of knowledge.

Secondly, there needs to be effective communication between schools and pupils with SEND and their parents...

Effective communication between teachers from different school phases can be achieved by arranging regular visits by secondary teachers to primary school and, in return, visits by primary teachers to secondary school. These visits can take many forms including: Talks to pupils in assemblies and form time about their respective schools; taster lessons, especially opportunities for pupils to experience secondary school facilities such as science labs and design and technology workshops; teachers working together to plan lessons and discuss curriculum design, as well as observe each other in the classroom; teachers organising CPD sessions and teaching and learning conferences together, as well as professional dialogue and the dissemination of research findings and materials, and the sharing of good practice.

Effective communication with parents can be achieved by involving parents in a school's preparation for transition and by developing their understanding of the culture of the new school, helping them understand what to expect. In practice, this might include promoting
and enhancing the role of parent/carer partnerships suc h as through the use parent/ carer advisers.

It can also be achieved using parent voice mechanisms which gather, monitor and evaluate parental views in relation to transfers and transitions and give feedback and updates to parents ('You said, we did') showing how the school has listened to and responded to parents' questions and concerns.

Effective communication with pupils can be achieved by providing information about what to expect at each stage of the transfer process and where and who to go to for help or to have questions answered. It can also be achieved by ensuring that pupils are involved in the transition process at all stages, and are well informed of what to expect in their new school.

Thirdly, school visits and induction programmes which improve social and academic outcomes for pupils with SEND need to be given priority and invested in...

School visits work best when they are planned and publicised long before pupils transfer in order to give pupils and their parents/carers a good understanding of the new school and its systems and structures, expectations and routines.

Induction programmes also work best when the teachers involved are provided with appropriate training and detailed information about what they're expected to achieve. The induction also needs to be well structured and engaging with high quality resources. The planning and teaching of induction programmes needs to involve the core subjects of English, maths and science.

Ideally, prior to induction and as part of the school visits, pupils in primary schools should be enabled to make regular use of secondary school facilities in order to become familiar with secondary teachers, buildings and methods. Where daytime visits by primary pupils is not possible, after school clubs run by secondary teachers for pupils from their feeder primaries is a useful means of encouraging future pupils to become familiar with their new school prior to transfer.

Fourthly, transition needs to be differentiated for pupils with SEND because different pupils experience transfer in different ways and are differently able to cope with it...

In practice, this might take the form of identifying vulnerable pupils and assigning a dedicated teaching assistant to them to provide additional guidance and skills development. It might mean modifying the process for pupils with SEND, consulting educational psychologists, for example, about the emotional impact of life changes on vulnerable young people.

It might mean establishing dedicated summer schools for those pupils who are identified as at risk of falling behind at the start of the new academic year and continuing to work with them to ensure the gap does not widen in the intervening weeks between the end of Year 6 and the beginning of Year 7.

Fifthly, senior school leaders need to support the transition of pupils with SEND, and all staff need clearly defined roles and responsibilities...

In practice, this means that the headteacher and senior leadership team must provide their full support for the transition process - financially, in terms of resources, and psychologically. There needs to be a designated senior leader responsible for transition with the status to give it importance and able to align these processes with wider school improvement priorities. There also needs to be a designated member of staff responsible for the transition of pupils with SEND.

This also means that all other school staff have clearly defined responsibilities for transition. For example, there will be a member of staff who is the school's named person responsible for meeting parents/carers who want to drop in and discuss issues. They will be another member of staff responsible for managing data on new pupils (including prior attainment at Key Stages 1 and 2, and teacher assessments). And there will be a member of staff responsible for listening and responding to pastoral issues amongst new pupils.

In terms of senior leaders 'putting their money where their mouths are' by allocating appropriate resources to enable a smooth and successful transition, this might mean timetabling experienced teachers in Year 7 and, where possible, making teaching assistants available to provide in-class support for the first half term immediately following transfer. TAs are particularly useful because they can contribute to assessment, support pupils with SEND, provide valuable insights into the needs of individual pupils and maintain established routines when they change classes with individual pupils.

Senior leaders can also play a vital role in ensuring that high quality data is available for every pupil joining a new school, and in establishing a clear strategic vision for strengthening transfers and transitions through the work of the governing body, self-evaluation and the school improvement plan. Senior leaders and other staff with responsibility for transition can aid the transition process by developing a transfer and transitions policy that aligns with the school improvement plan and contributes to raising standards and closing attainment gaps between identified groups. And, finally, they can engage with and contribute to local and national plans to share effective practice and develop consistency. Talking of sharing best practice...

Finally, schools and their staff need to share examples of what works for pupils with SEND...

The transfer and transition process can be further improved if examples of good practice are identified and disseminated. For example, schools could engage with local and national research evidence about various aspects of transfer, particularly how to help pupils with SEND.

Senior leaders, teachers and other adults who work with pupils with SEND and/or their families could engage in professional development activities including action research. And groups of schools could work together to build leadership capacity and develop a greater knowledge base by involving pupils and parents/carers in the monitoring, reviewing and planning process, and by strategically sharing effective practice.

In addition to the activities that schools engage in during the transition process, they need to provide additional support for pupils with SEND. For example, they might decide to appoint a Teaching Assistant who's dedicated to transition and whose job it is to support vulnerable pupils.

Let's consider what that TA might do in practice...

In the spring term of Year 5, the Teaching Assistant (TA) for Transition might visit feeder primary schools with a member of the Senior Leadership Team in order to meet staff, pupils and parents, and to outline their role and responsibilities. They might also articulate how vulnerable pupils have been identified, and what support will be offered and why.

During the spring term visits, the TA might also meet Year 6 teachers and take suggestions for further referrals. They might then establish their groups and book dates for the summer term.

In the summer term of Year 5, the TA might meet individual pupils in their primary school settings and take groups of pupils (say 6-8) on visits to their secondary school on several occasions over the course of the summer term.

These groups and visits may be mixed with pupils from other primary schools in order to help pupils make new friends. The programme might be based around concerns and issues raised by the children and what practical strategies will support them in secondary school and may also include some generic coping strategies and soft skills, for example...

- What is a friend/how to make friends
- Packing a bag the night before
- Avoiding bullies
- Who might be the most important person?
- What would I do if.........? (problem solving)
- What is Homework Club?
- Being a good listener
- Using your leisure time
- How do I make my work more successful?

In the autumn and spring terms of Year 6, the TA might continue to work with their identified children. If the initial groups were each from single primary schools, the TA might now decide to amalgamate some or all of them. The TA will continue to listen to pupils and be responsive to their concerns.

CHAPTER SIX
Transitions within Key Stage 3

As I've already argued, the secret to an effective Key Stage 3 is a better transition process, a better curriculum, better homework, and better use of data. In the first chapter of this book I examined why improving the transition between primary and secondary schools was so important. Earlier, I explained how to improve the transition process and what an effective transition might look like in practice. In this chapter I will turn my attention to transition in its wider sense because transition is not just about the move from Year 6 into Year 7, from one Key Stage to another. Indeed, it is about the various movements within a Key Stage, too; particularly from Year 7 into Year 8 which is often regarded as a stop-gap year. And it is also about establishing longer term, more sustainable cross-phase partnerships between primary and secondary schools in order to make transition feel seamless, smooth and natural.

Let's explore - by way of example - the transition of pupils from Year 7 into Year 8 though the same principles apply to pupils' transition into any year group...

Year 7 is new and exciting, if not a little daunting; Year 9 assumes a higher status because its curriculum often includes elective subjects, it comes at the end of a key stage and carries with it national tests (albeit now optional) and GCSE options or, in some schools, signals the start of a three-year Key Stage 4. Year 8, however, which is awkwardly sandwiched between them, is often seen as a stop-gap, wandering alone and confused in the wilderness.

In Year 8 there are no tests of any great import, no big decisions to make, and nothing is particularly new or exciting anymore. New school is now old hat. What's more, it's often the year in which pupils' hormones begin to rage. As a result, towards the end of Year 7 and during Year 8, pupils begin to get demotivated and their progress slows or stalls.

If you Google 'Year 8 dip' you'll find plenty of frustrated patter in parents' forums as mums and dads ask if it's normal for their son or daughter to be so demotivated at school and to be stalling in their studies. The responses they garner are invariably reassuring: yes, it's perfectly normal and a perennial problem in schools. But aside from the chatroom chatter, there is precious little research or advice on how to tackle this phenomenon. So how can we avoid this 'dip'?

Well, as is often the case, I find the solution lies in the problem. If the problem is that Year 8 isn't regarded as new or exciting, then we need to make it feel new and exciting. If the problem is that Year 8 is the year in which pupils usually start puberty and their hormones kick in with a vengeance as they begin the journey towards maturity, then we need to recognise this increasing maturity. If the problem is that Year 8, without tests and options, is regarded as meaningless, as a stop-gap, then we need to make it feel meaningful and use assessment and feedback to motivate pupils to make better progress.

So here are my top tips for avoiding the Year 8 'dip' and ensuring that the transition from Year 7 into Year 8 is just as smooth and effective as we hope the transition from primary to secondary proved to be...

Make each year special and have a curriculum that ensures progression and continuity. We need to ensure that Year 8 is different to Year 7 and Year 9, that it offers something unique, challenging and engaging. This might be in the form of cross-curricular project-based learning but whatever approach to the curriculum we take we must make sure that Year 8 represents a significant step-change in terms of difficulty and complexity.

Notwithstanding the importance of spaced practice (of repeating learning several times and leaving increasingly long gaps before returning to re-test), what Year 8 must not do is unnecessarily repeat curriculum content from primary school and Year 7. In order to ensure Year 8 offers something new, Year 7 and Year 8 teachers, if they are different, must closely liaise on their curriculum planning to achieve continuity.

Another way to make Year 8 feel special is to take advantage of the freedom afforded by its lack of formal testing and qualifications and pack it full of extra-curricular opportunities such as educational visits, residential trips, and so on. Serve a rich diet of culture - in or out of school - with theatre productions and museum visits, healthy eating expos and sporting events, science fairs and art and design competitions and exhibitions. Really bring learning to life.

Of course, money is always a consideration but we must take Ofsted's advice and make better use of the Pupil Premium funding in Key Stage 3 rather than stockpile it for Key Stage 4 interventions. If we use more of it in Year 8 (and therefore less at GCSE) - in conjunction with other funding streams - in order to ensure that all pupils get fair access to enrichment opportunities, then they will be motivated and make better progress, hence they will commence their GCSEs from a more advantageous starting point and far fewer remedial interventions will be needed in Years 10 and 11.

Recognise the increasing maturity of pupils. We need to ensure that pupils - who are starting to experience puberty and grow into young adults - feel that their increasing maturity is being recognised and appreciated.

To do this, we need to make Year 8 pupils feel set apart from Year 7 but only in the best sense. Rather than setting Year 8 in opposition to Year 7 we should utilise their maturity and experience to support, advise and mentor the new cohort of pupils. Year 8 pupils could be trained as reading mentors, for example, or as break and lunchtime 'buddies' and guides. They could play a big role during the Year 7 induction.

We tend to favour much older pupils in these roles - and not without good reason as sixth form students are mature, more accomplished readers, and in need of supporting evidence for their UCAS applications - but older students are also busy with important exams whereas Year 8 have the time to spare and need to feel valued. They are also more able to empathise with their Year 7 peers, being closer in age and having more recently experienced transition and induction.

We could also recognise the increasing maturity of Year 8 pupils by tweaking our rewards and sanctions policy, ensuring that rewards remain age-appropriate and motivational, and that sanctions continue to be suitably punitive but not demeaning. Ideally, we should involve Year 8 pupils in this process by consulting them on what the rewards and sanctions should be - the very process of consultation, whatever the outcome, will make them feel valued and mature.

Have systems that recognise and correct disaffection early, and provide opportunities for a fresh start. As well as ensuring our rewards and sanctions policy remains relevant as pupils grow in maturity, we need to make sure that low-level disruption and general disaffection - which are prevalent in Year 8 - are spotted early and tackled effectively. Those systems need to be positive and motivating, giving pupils a reason to reassert themselves and work hard. The key, again, is in an effective rewards policy but also in the use of intrinsic rewards, the reward of learning itself not extrinsic rewards such as prizes.

In order for pupils to feel rewarded by learning and achieving, we need them to believe that their work has a genuine audience and purpose. Pupils also need to feel that they have some ownership of the work - both in terms of the content and format, and in terms of how it will be assessed.

Perhaps most importantly, any system that seeks to recognise and correct disaffection and low level disruption must make clear that there is a way back. Pupils need to be afforded a fresh start. This applies to pupils who may have misbehaved or underachieved in Year 7 who now need to know - explicitly and implicitly - that Year 8 represents a new start for them and an opportunity to make amends, and to pupils who let themselves down during Year 8 but need a way back before they start Year 9.

Have pastoral systems that support pupils in their learning as well as their behaviour. We need to make sure that our pastoral systems do not focus solely on pupils' behaviour and wellbeing - as is often the case in the early years of Key Stage 3. We must not neglect pupils' academic needs. In practice, this means providing support for pupils whose behaviour is good but who need support either over the long-term or at key waypoints on their learning journey. This might be in the form of in-class support or extra sessions, or it might be in the form of differentiated learning such as differentiated questioning, a choice of outcomes or the application of mastery learning approaches.

Regularly evaluate progress and have effective intervention plans. We need to ensure that Year 8 isn't a wasted year filled with 'fluff' assignments and meaningless assessments. We need to set meaningful work that will stretch and challenge pupils and then assess their progress regularly and accurately so that they can be given detailed formative feedback on which they can act and improve. In short, we should ensure that we put in place the same robust assessment, monitoring and tracking systems in Year 8 that we use for our GCSE and A Level students.

In practice, this means that pupil progress is regularly observed and analysed and that the data is shared with all interested parties - parents, staff and governors. This means that the data is used in several ways including to identify underperforming groups, to direct the appropriate deployment of staff and resources, to inform target-setting, to monitor the impact of strategies and interventions, and to challenge the aspirations and assumptions of pupils, parents and staff. This also means having in place a well-developed pupil tracking system to capture a wider range of data in addition to attainment levels, and using external data and self-evaluation in order to focus on gaps and progress, not just average attainment. And it means that attainment data, as well as informing staff on pupil progress, is used to provide pupils with regular feedback on their progress.

CHAPTER SEVEN
Cross-phase partnerships

Making a pupil's transition from Key Stage 2 to Key Stage 3 smooth and effective takes more than just a little team-work at the end of Year 6 and the beginning of Year 7. Indeed, even starting the process in Year 5 as I suggested earlier is not really sufficient. Rather, what is needed is long-term, genuine and sustainable collaboration between schools. We need early years, primary and secondary schools to work in close partnership on all aspects of a child's education, sharing information and resources, to ensure that each child is well-protected and experiences a continuity of service and support.

Why do we need better collaboration? Because projects that link up pupils, teachers and schools across early years, primary and secondary phases can have a positive impact on pupils and teachers by supporting pupils to experience a smoother transition and make continuous progress both academically and in terms of their soft skills, and by enabling teachers and schools to learn from best practice across different stages of the system.

So, what might this collaboration look like in practice? It might involve all phases of compulsory education establishing family links, sharing services such as family liaison officers, education welfare officers, SENCOs, EAL teachers and other specialists. It might involve all phases jointly planning and running projects and events such as summer schools or careers fairs. It might take the form of joint curriculum planning. It might take the form of joint CPD networks and INSET days, and teacher visits and exchanges. It might also involve cross-phase mentoring and tutoring.

Whatever form it takes in practice - and I will explore more examples in a moment - it is important, as much as is possible, to see the two phases as one, particularly to see Years 5 through to 8 as a single phase when it comes to planning the curriculum because this will help to bridge the primary/secondary divide. Planning a unique 'middle years' curriculum will also help to combat the problem of Key Stage 3 - particularly Year 8 - being seen as 'wasted years' and a poor relation to GCSE. Indeed, it will give it identify and purpose.

Whilst we're on this topic, what will also help to bridge the divide - and one of the desired outcomes of an effective cross-phase partnership - is encouraging pupils to bring in their best work from each subject in primary school when they start secondary. This work can then be affixed to the front of pupils' exercise books in Year 7 to remind them and their teachers what they're capable of producing. Such a tactic will help combat the common complaint that secondary teachers underestimate pupils' abilities and that pupils' standards slide following transition.

Another desired outcome of an effective cross-phase partnership is to ensure that all Year 6 and 7 teachers work together to familiarise each other with the National Curriculum of the phase they teach as well as the secondary school's own curriculum and the school curriculum for the main feeder primaries.

Cross-phase partnerships can also be fruitfully employed designing 'settling-in' sessions and summer schools for pupils but these should have an academic rather than pastoral flavour. Primary and secondary colleagues could also work together to design formative and summative assessment strategies which make it easier for teachers to track pupils' progress as they move out of one phase and into the next.

Where possible, cross-phase partnerships could enable teachers to work across the different phases in order to introduce more subject-specialist teaching to the later years of primary school as well as encourage a more holistic approach to pupils' development at the beginning of Key Stage 3.

Primary school leaders play a crucial role in making cross-phase partnerships work. Firstly, they need to set clear expectations for their staff about the importance of sharing and communicating with their secondary colleagues by encouraging teachers to help pupils produce transition 'passports' which showcase both their academic and their broader achievements at primary school. Secondary school leaders play an equally important role. For example, they need to encourage Year 7 teachers who are struggling to understand a particular pupil's needs to consider contacting their old Year 6 teacher for a conversation.

Multi-academy trusts that encompass secondaries and some of their feeder primaries have an advantage when it comes to cross-phase partnerships and many are already ahead of the curve. Their shared HR and payroll structures and systems enable greater and easier collaboration. For example, in cross-phase MATs it is possible to employ teachers who work across the primary and secondary phases. This might mean that Year 6 teachers move up with their classes and teach them in Year 7, thus making the transition much less daunting.

It is also possible to have cross-phase subject leaders so that, for example, a Director of English oversees the MAT's English provision from Reception right through to A Level and perhaps has a Subject Leader for each phase but the phases do not follow the traditional pattern but straddle the key stage divide such as the 'middle years' of Years 5 to 8. The same could be said of pastoral leaders, too, with a Pastoral Leader of Years 5, 6 and 7 rather than the traditional Key Stage 3. And senior leader roles could also be designed to ensure assessment, for example, as well as, say, the curriculum and pedagogy, are joined up and continuous across all phases.

In Wales, an experiment in cross-phase partnerships has led to improvements in pupil outcomes and the raising of standards of educational practice and attainment. NFER researchers analysed twenty schools – four matched pairs of secondary schools and six of primary schools - who were involved in the experiments in 2016 and found that most of the schools believed their partnerships had improved standards of teaching and learning, and had raised pupil performance in maths and numeracy.

The NFER also found evidence that leadership at both senior and middle levels had been enhanced because of cross-phase partnerships and that schools' data tracking and assessment systems had been strengthened.

Most of the staff who were interviewed noted the positive impact of the partnerships, and particularly praised the "mutual trust, willingness and respect between the schools which had facilitated effective collaboration". However, they also admitted that there were some factors which might have constrained the relationships, including proximity and differences in pupils, cohorts and characteristics.

One headteacher involved in the project told NFER researchers: "The key for us in the beginning was trust and we are now in the situation where we are very open with each other, friendly ... it was about developing relationships, going slowly, getting to know each other and having the confidence to be open and honest."

Teachers who were involved in the project reported that they had refined approaches to teaching and learning, which had had a big impact on the work done. Teachers felt more confident to try different approaches and to experiment with techniques that they may not have used previously. Thus, lessons become more dynamic and interactive, inviting pupils to become active participants. The quality of feedback improved and teachers changed the way they asked questions, allowing them to elicit answers which delved into how well learners understood concepts and issues.

Some schools had also used the partnerships to look at how they might deliver the curriculum more effectively, including focusing on literacy and numeracy. Teachers told the NFER that being involved in a partnership had made them more reflective of their own practice, and that they had looked at different ways of learning. This included examining how they used data as part of teaching and learning to suit the individual needs of classes of individual pupils.

In secondary schools, most heads and teachers said that participation in the partnership had had a positive effect on teaching, with one senior leader describing it as a "journey of improvement". Teachers said that they had more opportunities to self-evaluate their own classroom practice and were developing an "extended repertoire of teaching, assessment and tracking skills". This was achieved by discussing different methods and approaches, sharing schemes of work and methods of tracking and using data, as well as lesson observations. Teachers also said they had gained the skills to teach smaller classes and of working with individual pupils.

The NFER report said: "Most senior leaders and teachers considered that classroom practice was improving because of the increased interaction between staff within and between schools, which had raised staff awareness of alternative approaches when planning, teaching and assessing."

At the whole-school level, one primary or secondary school in the partnership often influenced how things were done in the other. Headteachers became more reflective of their own leadership styles and in some cases, leadership teams were restructured because of the partnership. There were also changes among some middle leadership teams, with some middle leaders taking on new responsibilities.

The use of data was also strengthened, with schools changing how they collected data and how they then used this to support teaching and learning, in supporting individual pupils. NFER researchers noted that in some partnerships staff raised their expectations of what learners could achieve. At the same time, pupils were made more aware of their targets and the level at which they should be working. This had the knock-on effect of making them reflect on their own needs, even setting down their own success criteria. Partnership schools used pupils' work from both settings to standardise judgments for assessment and moderation. In some cases, work from one school was adapted for use in the other.

However, what did not work was an approach based on transferring practice directly from one school to another, or where school leaders assumed that what worked in their school would be effective practice elsewhere. As a result of all this, the NFER found that: "Learners' motivation improved and they were more engaged with teachers and the learning process. These changes were related to work to strengthen learners' voices, through formal processes for them to make their views known about their own learning and other work to nurture their independence and their enjoyment of their work."

The most lasting changes, researchers found, came about when there was a shift in attitude and culture, and this was needed alongside structural and procedural changes if reforms were to work.

The partnerships appear to have helped schools to make sustained improvements. The study concluded that the partnerships had been effective in supporting and speeding up changes in participating schools. This was achieved partly through matching up schools effectively, the support that was given by the government, and the 'emotional intelligence' shown by senior leaders in getting their staff on board with the project while being mindful of their emotions and sensibilities.

Part Three

Making Curriculum Count

CHAPTER EIGHT
Curriculum collaboration

One of the advantages of the kinds of cross-phase partnership I explored in Chapter Seven is the opportunity for primary and secondary colleagues to collaborate on curriculum planning in order to ensure a joined-up approach so that work is not repeated. Another way of ensuring the curriculum flows between the two phases - and one I mentioned briefly in Chapter Three - is for primary and secondary teachers to design a 'bridging unit' that links the end of Year 6 with the beginning of Year 7. This has several advantages. Not only do pupils see the explicit link between the two phases and therefore feel less daunted by the perceived 'divide' between the two, they are also able to start the new year at an advantage, with prior knowledge of a subject and with ready-made work to show their new teacher what they're capable of achieving.

Another advantage of cross-phase partnerships related to the curriculum is the opportunity to share data in order to ensure that pupils' prior attainment is used to set groups and to plan teaching so that lessons provide appropriate challenge. This helps avoid the common criticism that Year 7 often repeats work that pupils did in Year 6 or is too easy. And it helps Year 7 teachers to differentiate effectively.

But data is more than just a spreadsheet, it is a conversation...

Most secondary teachers will already have access to some information about their new Year 7s including which primary school they came from, the scaled scores they achieved on their Key Stage 2 tests and, if they delve into the question level analysis available, the marks they received for individual questions in those tests. But a pupil's Year 6 teacher will know so much more than these numbers can possibly tell us. They'll know, for example, what the pupil can achieve when they're not under test conditions and what topics they've studied and found interesting. They'll know what their attitude to learning is like and what skills they've developed over their first seven years of schooling. They'll know what extra-curricular activities they've taken part in and how well they did, as well as what motivates them to succeed and what demotivates them. They'll know, too, what their home life is like and what obstacles they've had to overcome and might still be facing daily.

So, yes, data is more than a spreadsheet. And cross-phase partnerships and shared curriculum planning enables data to become a rich and meaningful conversation.

As well as what is taught, cross-phase partnerships can ensure that - when it comes to the curriculum - teachers from primary and secondary schools liaise on how it is taught. A partnership might, for example, set up a primary/secondary CPD network to ensure that approaches to pedagogy are better matched and that teachers from both phases learn from each other about what works in the classroom and about what motivates pupils and how pupils learn. It's important for teachers on both sides of the transition 'divide' to remember that the learning flows both ways: primary and secondary teachers have a lot to learn from each other when it comes to pedagogy and practice.

Moving away from cross-phase partnerships and focusing solely on secondary schools, the most important message for secondary leaders when looking to improve their Key Stage 3 curriculum - and by so doing, academic achievement in Years 7, 8 and 9 - is that Key Stage 3 is a springboard to GCSE success. As such, it must not be regarded as a poor relation to Key Stage 4 for this will only prove to be a self-fulfilling prophecy.

In practice, this means school leaders - particularly the school timetabler - should avoid the temptation to schedule Key Stages 4 and 5 first then fill in the gaps with Key Stage 3 lessons, thus increasing the chances of Key Stage 3 classes being split between two or more teachers. It also means avoiding timetabling non-specialist, underperforming and/or inexperienced teachers for Key Stage 3 lessons, especially in the core subjects and other EBacc subjects. School leaders should utilise their best teachers because this will pay dividends in later years and avoid having to employ remedial interventions to help pupils catch up for lost time.

As well as ensuring that Key Stage 3 lessons are appropriately staffed, the curriculum needs to strike the right balance between providing pupils with a grounding for GCSE and being different enough to Key Stage 4 to be engaging. To make Key Stage 3 stand out as unique, you might consider taking advantage of the freedom it offers by contemplating project-based learning and a focus on developing pupils' metacognition and self-regulation skills, for example by employing cooperative learning activities.

Rest assured I'm not suggesting you ditch the traditional academic curriculum and teach something woolly that results in lots of posters and role play. But I am suggesting that you try to teach the curriculum in a way that's different to GCSE and in a way that helps pupils to become their own teachers, to engage in cooperative learning activities and to take ownership of their studies. And there's no shortage of evidence that this approach works. For example, metacognition and self-regulation are ranked number one in the Sutton Trust/Education Endowment Foundation table of educational effectiveness. And John Hattie, in his book 'Visible Learning' (2009), said that "The biggest effects on student learning occur when teachers become learners of their own teaching, and when students become their own teachers".

CHAPTER NINE
Learning environment

Once we've achieved greater curriculum continuity, we need to enable pupils to access it by building a positive learning environment because, as research by the University of Salford suggests, emotional and physiological stability can directly impact on pupils' understanding of the school curriculum and, therefore, affect the pace of their progress. And this is no more important than in the aftermath of pupils' transition from primary to secondary school when they are most vulnerable.

Creating an environment that allows pupils to feel comfortable, content and focused, therefore, can help pupils become more attentive to their teacher and more attuned to the content of the curriculum they are studying.

In other words, pupils' conscious and subconscious attentions, and the development of their knowledge, skills and understandings are more effectively piqued when they study in a positive learning environment.

So, what exactly is a positive learning environment?

The University of Salford study suggests that a wide range of environmental factors can contribute towards the emotional and physiological effects of a classroom. For example, environmental factors including natural light, noise, classroom orientation, temperature and even air quality have been shown to improve pupils' achievement by as much as 25% in an academic year.

Salford also found that over 70% of the variations in pupil performance could be directly attributed to environmental factors.

And emotional factors can be just as significant as physical ones when it comes to pupils' academic progress. Creating a sense of safety, therefore, is one of the most impactful steps teachers can take towards improving pupils' capacity to learn and their intellectual understanding of the curriculum.

What's more, the first few days spent in a new learning environment (in other words, in the early stages of Year 7) are the most pivotal in determining a pupil's academic progress. Indeed, we've already seen that almost 40% of pupils fail to make expected progress following their transition from primary to secondary school. If a pupil does not feel emotionally safe and intellectually comfortable, it can prove difficult for them to make progress.

Of course, classrooms should always be a safe place for children wherein they feel supported physically, emotionally and academically. This support comes not just from teachers, but also from their peers, support staff, and - as we've just seen - from the physical classroom itself.

An intelligently-designed learning environment with, for example, distinct and clear lines of communication can help promote dialogue between pupils and teachers. This, in turn, can help pupils to feel better integrated in the learning process which, in turn, helps promote wellbeing within the classroom.

Dr Victoria Revell, a chronobiologist at the University of Surrey, argues that "Light is critical for our health and wellbeing. Ensuring that we receive adequate light levels at the appropriate time of day benefits our alertness, mood, productivity, sleep patterns and many aspects of our physiology."

Furthermore, the use of colour in the classroom can affect pupils' moods and emotional wellbeing. Ancient Chinese and Egyptian civilisations practiced early arts of chromotherapy which involved the use of colours as therapy and emotional healing, a practice that is still widely used today.

The learning environment for pupils with SEND and those vulnerable during transition

Creating a positive learning environment, then, is crucial for ensuring every pupil makes progress but environmental factors become even more critical to pupils' success when those pupils have SEND or are particularly vulnerable during times of change...

According to a 2014 report by the charity Mencap, 65% of parents of children with SEND believed their child had received a poorer quality of education than their peers without SEND, in large part because their child had sometimes been removed from the classroom and taught separately, but also because the main classroom had not been adjusted to meet their needs.

In 2013, the University of London's Institute of Education reported that pupils with SEND were routinely segregated from their teachers and classmates, spending more than a quarter of their time in school away from qualified teachers and the classroom.

What's more, when pupils with SEND are taken out of their normal classrooms, they tend to be housed in smaller rooms that are not conducive to learning. It is not atypical, for example, for these pupils to be taught (either in small groups or on the basis of one-to-one tuition) in rooms which have ill-matched and broken tables and chairs, and which were designed for other purposes such as the dining hall, library, computer room, and staff offices.

These rooms by their nature are often adjacent to busy or noisy spaces, such as staff rooms, playgrounds or corridors, and have become dumping grounds for unused stationery or broken equipment.

Sometimes, these rooms are also poorly ventilated or heated, and have little natural light.

Both the Teacher Standards (2012) and the SEND Code of Practice (2014) require teachers to ensure all the pupils in their classes can access learning, and this - it is made explicitly clear - means adapting their learning environment, for example by providing visual timetables, writing frames and mind-maps, or by providing physical resources such as sloped writing boards.

Pupils with SEND also tend to respond best when the classroom is tidy and organised, when the teacher sits with the pupil at the front of the class and provides differentiated handouts which summarise and clarify the key points from the lesson rather than expecting pupils to copy copiously from the board.

The best learning environments have a range of resources such as personalised dictionaries, writing frames, lists of sentence starters, lists of linking words, mini-whiteboards and coloured pens, pastel coloured paper and notebooks, aide memoire to support individual learning activities, and tailored handouts to support specific tasks.

Pupils who are susceptible to visual stress are best supported by coloured overlays, cream paper for handouts and exercise books, pastel or cream backgrounds on computer screens and PowerPoint presentations, a font size no smaller than 12 point for paper and 28 point for PowerPoint, texts in a sans serif font such as Arial, Verdana, and Tahoma, left-justified text, and the use of bold to emphasise text but the avoidance of italics, underlining and capitals.

Classroom displays work best for pupils with SEND when they are informative, interactive and relevant, are uncluttered so that key information can quickly and easily be found, and can be seen from every position in the classroom. Displays also work best when there is a good use of colour, when they contain key words that are explicitly taught to and understood by all pupils and then frequently referenced in lessons, and when they celebrate pupils' work and make them feel valued.

Classrooms that work best for pupils with SEND are also:

1. Suitably adapted to the needs of pupils with SEND
2. Quiet and distraction-free
3. Fitted with good lighting, heating and ventilation
4. Visually attractive and inspiring
5. Stocked with requisite resources and equipment, all within easy reach of pupils and adults including, for example, a white board, flip chart, and writing resources, but which is also clutter-free.
6. Equipped with the appropriate furniture and space, including chairs and a table at the right height.

I hope I've said little with which to disagree so far but is this all? Surely there's more than this to creating a positive learning environment that supports pupils during and immediately after transition to secondary school and that is adapted to the needs of pupils with SEND? Most of the features I list above are related to the physical environment, after all. And isn't a classroom more than just the bricks and mortar of the built environment? Surely a positive learning environment is also about how the teacher teaches and about the culture or ethos they create?

The SEND Code of Practice says that 'Special educational provision is underpinned by high quality teaching and is compromised by anything less.' Providing an inclusive learning environment whereby pupils' needs are met without drawing attention to their difficulties, therefore, is crucial because this will maximise their learning potential but limit any feelings they may have of embarrassment and frustration.

As such, let's now turn our attentions to some of the pedagogical and emotional - rather than physical - features of a positive learning environment...

In a moment, we will consider some specific teaching strategies, but first I'd like us to take a step back and ask ourselves the ostensibly simple question: What is learning? It may seem like a simple question but it's not easy to answer because it's hard to do justice to what is, in truth, a complex, nuanced process. What's more, learning is often intangible, hard to pin down. Something happens in the brain but we're not sure exactly what and can't always see or know what's changed.

John Hattie says that learning is "the process of developing sufficient surface knowledge to then move to deeper understanding such that one can appropriately transfer this learning to new tasks and situations". Paul Kirschner, meanwhile, says learning is "a change in long-term memory". Paul Black and Dylan Wiliam, for their part, believe that learning is "an increase, brought about by experience, in the capacities of an organism to react in valued ways in response to stimuli". And Sonderstrom and Bjork think that learning creates "relatively permanent changes in comprehension, understanding, and skills of the types that will support long-term retention and transfer".

Learning, it seems, is even more complex and nuanced than first thought, made more complex for pupils with SEND who have a range of different learning needs, experience a variety of barriers to learning, and demonstrate their learning in many ways. Although all the definitions of learning I share above contain a common thread - namely, that something must happen in the long-term memory - each has a slightly different take and yet none of them is, well, satisfactory.

Perhaps Dan Willingham is right when he says we "ought not to worry overmuch about definitions". After all, learning can be a range of different things depending on its purpose and context, and can encompass different processes, procedures and indeed outcomes. For example, learning my telephone number is not the same as learning to ride a bike which, in turn, is not the same as learning how to analyse a poem or interpret a set of raw data and present the findings in a scatter graph.

In short, learning is multi-faceted, and the number of faces is greater when we're exploring the learning needs of pupils who are vulnerable during transition from primary to secondary school and those with SEND.

At its simplest, the process of learning is the interaction between one's sensory memory (sometimes referred to as our 'environment') and one's long-term memory. Our sensory memory is made up of: what we see - this is called our iconic memory; what we hear - this is called our echoic memory; and what we touch - our haptic memory. Our long-term memory is where new information is stored and recalled but we cannot directly access it. As such, the interaction between our sensory memory and our long-term memory must take place in our working memory, or short-term memory, which is the only place where we can think and do.

To stimulate pupils' sensory memories and thus engage the attention of their working memories and make them think, we need to create an environment that is conducive to learning and that stimulates pupils' iconic, echoic and haptic memories.

As such, as well as possessing the physical features I mention above, an effective learning environment is, to my mind, one in which, emotionally, all pupils:

- Feel welcomed,
- Feel valued,

- Are enthusiastic about learning,
- Are engaged in their learning,
- Are eager to experiment, and
- Feel rewarded for their hard work.

Behind all these characteristics is a simple - though oxymoronic - aim: to ensure pupils are comfortable with discomfort.

In other words, we want pupils to know that the work they'll be asked to do in our classrooms will be tough, that they will be challenged with hard work and made to think hard. We want pupils to know that there will be no hiding place in our classrooms; they must ask and answer questions and attempt everything we ask of them. We differentiate by outcome not by task, and we certainly do not lower our expectations. We have high aspirations for every pupil in our class and support every pupil to succeed.

However, in so doing, we want them to feel safe and protected, we want them to be eager to face challenge, and to willingly attempt hard work because they know we've strung a safety net beneath them: they might fall but we will catch them. We want them to know that taking risks and making mistakes is not just accepted in our classrooms but is positively and proactively welcomed as an essential part of the learning process. Indeed, the only people who don't make mistakes either don't get any better at anything or have reached the point of automaticity - they have fully mastered something and so can now do it through habit.

Our pupils are not at the point of automaticity and so must make mistakes if they are to get better at anything. If they don't make mistakes, they cannot receive feedback; if they don't receive feedback, they will not know how to improve; if they don't know how to improve, they simply won't improve.

John Hattie says, "A teacher's job is not to make work easy. It is to make it difficult. If you are not challenged, you do not make mistakes. If you do not make mistakes, feedback is useless."

There are many ways of achieving a positive learning environment in which pupils are comfortable with discomfort: some are simple, some more complex....

For example, a teacher could establish a habit of greeting pupils at the classroom door at the start of every lesson, smiling as pupils enter and welcoming at least some of them by name. A teacher could ensure they're on time and have a lesson planned and ready to go. They could model enthusiasm by constantly articulating - through their words and actions - their joy at teaching these pupils and at teaching their subject. Sometimes a little over-acting goes a long way. It's better to be considered the kooky, eccentric teacher who's truly, madly, deeply in love with science, say, than the boring, staid one who never cracks a smile and only perseveres for the pension.

Finally, a teacher could establish a growth mindset culture in which effort is prized over attainment, hard work is rewarded, and mistakes are shared and celebrated.

CHAPTER TEN
Cooperative learning

So far in this section of the book on making the curriculum count, we've considered ways of ensuring there is greater continuity between primary and secondary schools in terms of what is taught. We've also looked at ways of creating a positive learning environment that supports pupils, particularly those who are vulnerable during transition or have SEND, immediately following a change of schools. Now let's turn our attention to *how* the curriculum is taught...

Broadly speaking, classroom learning activities can be either competitive, individualistic, or co-operative. Competitive learning is where pupils compete for marks to see who the best is. Individualistic learning is where pupils work more independently of each other and, perhaps, of the teacher.

So, what, then, is cooperative learning...?

Firstly, what it is not: cooperative learning is not simply synonymous with group work. Rather, cooperative learning is where pupils are required to work together as they learn and have a vested interest in each other's learning. And it's proven to work...

Cooperative learning is, according to the research, the most effective of the three types of learning in terms of academic performance and classroom climate. What's more, cooperative learning can improve pupils' achievement by at least one grade according to John Hattie's meta-analysis of the evidence.

Put simply, cooperative learning refers to those teaching methods which are structured in such a way as to achieve three characteristics thought to enhance learning. Namely, that:

1. Groups succeed or fail together - in other words, individual pupils are held accountable by their peers and peer pressure is used constructively to motivate pupils to learn.

2. Pupils work interactively - in other words, activities involve peer teaching and intensive pupil-led group discussions.

3. One of the lesson objectives is for pupils to learn as part of a team and to help others learn - in other words, groups become motivated to help the weakest members so that the group as a whole performs better. Pupils have a vested interest in each other's success: they only succeed if they all succeed; if one fails, they all fail.

An integral element of this model of cooperative learning is that pupils are held accountable by their teacher for learning and working effectively as a group and for supporting each other to learn. Therefore, as a consequence, pupils come to learn how to work together and to cooperate with each other.

Metacognition

The term metacognition means 'cognition about cognition' or, more informally, 'thinking about thinking'.

The American developmental psychologist John H. Flavell defined metacognition as knowledge about cognition and control of cognition. For example, a person engages in a process of metacognition if she notices that she is having more trouble learning X than Y; or if it strikes her that she should double-check Z before accepting it as a fact.

Metacognition also involves thinking about your own processes of cognition such as study skills, memory capabilities, and the ability to monitor your own learning. Metacognition needs to be explicitly taught along with subject content.

Metacognitive knowledge is about your own cognitive processes and your understanding of how to regulate those processes in order to maximize your learning.

Metacognitive knowledge includes:

- Content knowledge (declarative knowledge) – in other words, understanding your own capabilities such as evaluating your own knowledge of a topic.
- Task knowledge (procedural knowledge) – in other words, understanding how you perceive the difficulty of a task.
- Strategic knowledge (conditional knowledge) – in other words, understanding how capable you are of using strategies to learn information.

Metacognition is a general term encompassing the study of memory-monitoring and self-regulation, meta-reasoning, consciousness/awareness and auto-consciousness/self-awareness. These capacities are used to maximise your potential to think and to learn.

In practice, to help pupils develop metacognition, we need to give them time to foster understanding and time to reflect on their learning. Reflection might involve pupils rethinking their grasp of important ideas, perhaps with the teacher's guidance. It might involve pupils improving their work through revision based on self-assessment and feedback. It might involve pupils reflecting on their learning and performance.

A linear path through the curriculum content (i.e. teaching it once then moving on) is a mistake. After all, how can pupils master complex ideas and tasks if they encounter them only once? Therefore, the flow of learning must be iterative, pupils must be made fully aware of the need to rethink and revise in light of current learning, and the work must follow the trail back to the original big idea and learning goal.

Let's take an example...

In a Key Stage 3 humanities lesson pupils might explore the big question 'What is democracy?' by discussing their experiences and by reading various texts about democracy. Pupils might then develop a theory of democracy and create a concept map for the topic. The teacher might then cause them to rethink their initial ideas by raising a second big question, using an appropriate example: 'What is representative democracy and majority rule - and how does it work?' The pupils might then modify their concept of democracy as they come to understand that democracy can sometimes feel disenfranchising and unfair if most voters do not share your own beliefs and values and if your own MP votes against their constituents' wishes.

As illustrated in this example, in-built rethinking and reflection is a critical and deliberate element of metacognition and self-regulation; moreover, it's central to learning for understanding. We must, therefore, ensure our Key Stage 3 lessons provide opportunities for pupils to constantly reconsider their earlier understandings of the big ideas we've taught them if they are ever to get beyond simplistic thinking and to the heart of the kind of deep understanding that's now required in Key Stage 4 and beyond. Talking of 'beyond'...

The most successful people in life have the capacity to self-monitor and self-adjust as needed. They proactively consider what is working, what isn't, and what might be done better. Another aspect of reflection, therefore, is self-assessment. Here, it is worth considering how pupils will engage in some form of self-evaluation (in order to identify any remaining questions and to set future targets), and how pupils will be helped to take stock of what they have learned and what needs further inquiry or refinement.

Pupils need to be afforded opportunities to self-monitor, self-assess, and self-adjust their work, individually and collectively, as the work progresses. Central to this kind of self-understanding is an honest self-assessment, based on increasing clarity about what we do understand and what we don't; what we have accomplished and what remains to be done.

Crucially, the kind of internal dialogue that's critical to metacognition needs to be explicitly taught; it's not innate. When we look at the 'conditions for learning' in a moment I will explore some practical ways in which we can teach metacognition.

Enquiry-based learning

Both cooperative learning and metacognition involve planning for effective collaborative learning. This means the explicit teaching of communication skills, as well as thinking and reasoning skills.

One possible model for delivering this in the classroom is to get pupils engaging in a project every half-term which is allocated one lesson per week on the timetable. The project might alternate between an individual and a group task. It might be organised on themes allowing a certain degree of autonomy over its content and format.

Where enquiry-based learning of this nature is used, it is important that projects inspire and challenge pupils, are predicated on the idea of every pupil succeeding, and involve genuine research. It is also important that projects have in-built flexibility to allow for a range of abilities, are broken into clear components, and make clear what is expected of each pupil at each stage of their development, thus spelling out the qualities and dimensions on which the work will eventually be judged.

Teachers need to foster a sense of whole-class pride in the quality of learning and ensure that, once finished, project work is made public – providing a genuine audience. Project assessments should be used as the primary context for sharing knowledge and skills and this means teaching pupils how to give constructive feedback - another important skill they will need for GCSE and beyond. Finally, teachers need to instil in their pupils the belief that quality means rethinking, reworking, and polishing so that they feel celebrated, not ridiculed, for going back to the drawing board.

Pupils might also be allowed to choose their own talk partners and small groups at the start of Year 7 then their teachers might choose the groups later in the year. Conflicts might be resolved using restorative justice.

There might be a focus on communication skills throughout the year. Ground rules for group talk might be co-constructed with pupils then displayed in the classroom and regularly revisited.

Pupils may complete reflective learning journals once a fortnight that focus on how they learn and what barriers they face, and how they can overcome them.

Whatever approach is taken, Key Stage 3 is an ideal time to think creatively about the timetable and about finding ways of challenging and engaging pupils in ways that will help them grow as learners and develop the skills - as well as the knowledge - they will need at GCSE and beyond.

One skill they will need - and, I would argue, one key aspect of metacognition and self-regulation - is transfer, the ability to transfer what has been learnt in one context to other contexts. Perkins & Salomon (1989) identified two mechanisms through which the transfer of knowledge and skills could take place: Low road transfer (in which a skill is practised to near automaticity); and high road transfer (in which transfer relies on the deliberate mindful abstraction of an underlying principle). Pintrich & de Groot (1990), meanwhile, identified the importance of motivation in transfer ('children need the will as well as the skill').

The importance of self-regulation in promoting such transfer became increasingly recognised at the turn of the century (e.g. Schunk & Ertmer 2000) while Watkins (2001) defined effective transfer as requiring 1. Requisite skills, 2. Choosing to use the skills, 3. Recognising when a skill is appropriate in new situations, and 4. Metacognitive awareness, monitoring and checking progress. In short, using Key Stage 3 to help pupils develop the ability to self-regulate will help them to transfer their learning at later stages of their education, thus making their learning universal and therefore meaningful. In other words, it will provide them with the springboard to success at GCSE and beyond.

CHAPTER ELEVEN
Motivation

Let's stay with the subject of *how* the Key Stage 3 curriculum is taught and consider the conditions we need to put in place in Years 7, 8 and 9 in order for pupils to learn effectively...

Occasionally, on my teacher-training courses and when the mood takes me, I ask colleagues to draw a picture of something familiar, something a child might doodle. A boat. A lighthouse. A car. An island. A house.

I give them five minutes and ask them to work alone and in silence. When the five minutes are up, I ask them to swap their drawings with the person next to them so they can peer-assess their artwork. And at this point I share the assessment criteria.

If I'd asked colleagues to draw a house, say, I might at this stage inform them that if they've included a front door they can have five points. If they've drawn a path leading up to that front door, they can be awarded a further five points. If they have five or more windows, each with curtains, they can add another five marks to their tally. A chimney with two chimney pots gets them another five; a garage, five points; a driveway with a car parked on it, five points; and so on.

Delegates then calculate their partner's total score and equate this to a grade before handing it back. It's rare for anyone to get an A or a B. More often than not, colleagues get a D or an E.

Although, by the time they've finished sharing their grades with the class, colleagues have already begun to discern one moral of the story - that we must share the assessment criteria with pupils before we set an assignment and we must only assess work using the criteria we make explicit beforehand - I move on from the task without further comment in order to let this realisation (or consolidation of prior knowledge) ruminate.

Next I ask delegates to think of something they're good at and to think about how they became good at it. I then ask them how they know they are good at it - on what evidence is this judgment based?

I ask delegates to think of something they're not very good at and to consider why - what went wrong when they were trying to learn this thing and who, if anyone, was to blame? I then ask them to think about something they are good at now but didn't initially want to learn. What kept them going in lieu of motivation?

Finally, I ask colleagues to think of a time they've helped someone - ideally not a pupil in a school setting, but perhaps a friend or family member - to learn something. To what extent, I ask them, did they understand the subject better once they'd taught it to someone else? And did assessing that person's learning help them to understand the subject even more deeply?

I then canvass colleagues' responses and our subsequent discussions almost always result in the following conclusions:

We decide that most people become good at things through practice, by learning from their mistakes, and by experimenting. People learn best when they engage in a process of trial and error and when they repeat their actions several times, making incremental improvements each time. As the Danish nuclear physicist, Niels Bohr once said, "[An expert is] someone who has made all the mistakes which it is possible to make in a very narrow field".

My colleagues and I also conclude that most people know they have a right to feel positive about their achievements because of evidence given in the form of feedback, particularly when they receive praise, and as a result of receiving a reward for doing well. People also know that they can feel positive about their achievements when they are asked to help others achieve the same end-goal and when they can see the results of their labours for themselves.

My colleagues and I conclude that, when learning fails, it's usually because the learner didn't engage in enough practice, didn't work hard enough or lacked focus. Perhaps the feedback the learner received was poor or else they did not act upon it, or at any rate did not act upon it in a timely manner. Perhaps the communication between the teacher and the learner was poor. More often than not, though, learning fails when the learner lacks sufficient motivation, when they simply aren't interested in learning the thing being taught because it's not personally meaningful to them.

So, what, I ask my colleagues, in the absence of motivation - when pupils don't have the want to learn - keeps pupils going until they succeed? My colleagues and I usually conclude that it must be the need to learn - having a rationale, a necessity to learn, and therefore taking ownership of the learning - that keeps people going and helps them to overcome their lack of motivation to succeed.

My discussions with my teacher-training colleagues also conclude that by teaching something to a third party we learn more about it ourselves because the act of teaching enables us to gain feedback and make better sense of a topic. Teaching is also a form of learning by doing, of learning through practice. The fact we have to teach something to someone else also addresses the need to learn it (we have to learn it in order to teach it to someone else, after all) and we confront the want to learn all the time we are teaching - or indeed the lack of motivation.

Once we've taught something and we assess our pupils' learning to see if we've been successful, we learn it for ourselves even more deeply because we discover all the mistakes people can make and we discover all the different ways in which pupils can make sense of a topic. In short, we gain lots of feedback about how to teach the topic the next time. Assessing someone's learning is also another means of learning by doing. And assessing someone else's learning forces us to define and redefine the standards of pupils' achievements.

Piecing these discussions together, and reminding my teacher-training colleagues of the initial task whereby they drew a picture of a house without knowing the criteria on which they'd eventually be assessed, I share what I term 'the conditions for learning' - in other words, the state of affairs that must exist in order for our pupils to be able to learn effectively.

There are, to my mind, six conditions which must be in place in our classrooms in order for learning to happen. These are:

1. Intrinsic motivation
2. Purpose
3. Practice
4. Feedback
5. Metacognition
6. Assessment

Let's look at each of these six 'conditions for learning' in turn... In this chapter we'll focus on motivation, both in terms of intrinsic motivation - the desire to do something for the sake of doing it, and extrinsic motivation or purpose - the desire to do something because it leads to an external reward. In Chapter Twelve we'll look at practice, feedback, metacognition and assessment.

Condition for learning #1: Intrinsic motivation

In order to create the conditions for pupils to learn, we need to establish their want to learn - we need them to be motivated to learn. This involves them understanding why it matters that they learn what we intend to teach them.

Intrinsic motivation is the self-desire to seek out new things and new challenges, to gain new knowledge. Often, intrinsic motivation is driven by an inherent interest or enjoyment in the task itself, and exists within the individual rather than relying on external pressures or necessity.

Put simply, it's the desire to do something even though there is no reward except a sense of accomplishment at achieving that thing. Intrinsic motivation is a natural motivational tendency and is a critical element in cognitive, social, and physical development.

Pupils who are intrinsically motivated are more likely to engage in a task willingly as well as work to improve their skills, which will - in turn - increase their capabilities. Pupils are likely to be intrinsically motivated if they:

- attribute their educational results to factors under their own control, also known as autonomy
- believe in their own ability to succeed in specific situations or to accomplish a task - also known as a sense of self-efficacy
- are genuinely interested in accomplishing something to a high level of proficiency, knowledge and skill, not just in achieving good grades - also known as mastery.

Condition for learning #2: Purpose

In order to create the right conditions for pupils to learn, we need to establish their need to learn - we need them to have clear targets and to know why they need to learn what we intend to teach them and how they will use that learning later.

If the want to learn is concerned with intrinsic motivation, we might loosely argue that the need to learn - the purpose - is linked to extrinsic motivation...

Extrinsic motivation refers to the performance of an activity in order to attain a desired outcome and it is the opposite of intrinsic motivation. Extrinsic motivation comes from influences outside of the individual's control; a rationale, a necessity, a need. Common forms of extrinsic motivation are rewards (for example money or prizes), or - conversely- the threat of punishment.

We can provide pupils with a rationale for learning by sharing the 'big picture' with them. In other words, we can continually explain how their learning fits in to the module, the course, the qualification, their careers and to success in work and life. For example, we can explain how today's lesson connects with yesterday's lesson and how the learning will be extended or consolidated next lesson, as well as how it will be assessed at a later stage. We can explain how this learning will become useful in later life, too. And we can connect the learning in one subject with the learning in other subjects, making explicit the transferability of knowledge and skills and the interconnectedness of skills in everyday life.

This is not to suggest that pupils will possess either intrinsic or extrinsic motivation. Rather, it is desirable for pupils to possess or develop both. Pupils should both want and need to learn. However, it is natural that some pupils will lack the want to learn and so instilling in them the need to learn becomes more important.

However, a word of warning: the need to learn should be about explaining the rationale, outlining why acquiring the knowledge and skills you're teaching will be useful to pupils now and in the future, and it should be about showing pupils the big picture, connecting the learning. It should not be about using a carrot and a stick - rewards and sanctions - to motivate pupils because social psychological research has indicated that the use of extrinsic rewards has the potential to reduce the level of pupils' intrinsic motivation. In one study demonstrating this effect, for example, children who expected to be (and were indeed) rewarded with a ribbon and a gold star for drawing pictures spent less time playing with the drawing materials in subsequent observations than children who were assigned to an unexpected reward condition.

Having said this, the nature of the reward matters. For example, in another study pupils who were rewarded with a book demonstrated better reading behaviours in the future, implying that some rewards do not undermine intrinsic motivation and can be educationally beneficial.

In the bonus chapter at the end of this section of the book on project-based learning I will explain how to ensure a project has purpose. For example, I will explain that a project can fulfil an educational purpose if it provides opportunities to build metacognition and character skills such as collaboration, communication, and critical thinking, which will serve pupils well in the workplace as in life. A project can also fulfil an educational purpose if pupils conduct a real-life inquiry, rather than finding information in textbooks or on the Internet then making a poster. A project can also fulfil an educational purpose if it makes learning meaningful by emphasising the need to create high-quality products and performances through the formal use of feedback and drafting. And finally, a project can fulfil an educational purpose if it ends with a product being presented to a real audience.

But as well-being educationally meaningful, we need to make sure work is made personally meaningful. A project can be given a personal purpose if we begin by triggering pupils' curiosity. In other words, at the start of the first lesson on the project, we use a 'hook' to engage our pupils' interest and initiate questioning. A project can also be made personally meaningful to pupils if we pose a big question which captures the heart of the project in clear, compelling language, and which gives pupils a sense of purpose and challenge. And finally, a project can be made personally meaningful to pupils if they are given some choice about how to conduct the project and present their findings.

CHAPTER TWELVE
The open loop

.

In order to create the conditions for pupils to learn effectively, we need to ensure they are afforded opportunities to learn by doing, and to learn from their mistakes (what we call 'the open loop').

In Part Four of this book on homework, I will explore the importance of practice tasks in more detail. I will, for example, explain how practice builds proficiency and mastery. I will also share three forms of practice, namely:

1. Spaced repetition. This is where information is learnt initially then repeated several times at increasingly long intervals so that pupils get to the point of almost forgetting what they've learnt and have to delve into their long-term memories to retrieve their prior knowledge, thus strengthening those memories.

2. Retrieval practice. This is testing or quizzing (such as multiple choice) used not for the purposes of assessment but for reinforcement and to provide pupils with feedback information on what they know and don't yet know so that they can better focus their future studies.

3. Cognitive disfluency (otherwise known as desirable difficulties). This is a memory technique that makes learning 'stick' by placing artificial barriers in the way of pupils' initial learning. Doing this means that the process of encoding (learning something for the first time) is made harder so that the process of retrieval (recalling that learning later, say in a test) is made quicker and easier.

Condition for learning #3: Practice

The power of practice - of learning through a process of trial and error - has a foundation in neurochemistry...

Whenever we do something – think, move, read this book – our brain sends a signal (like an electric charge) along the neurones in our brains and through our nerve fibres to our muscles. In other words, every skill we possess – swinging a golf club, writing great fiction, playing the piano – is created by chains of nerve fibres carrying small electrical impulses like the signals travelling through a circuit. Each time we practise something, a different highly specific circuit is illuminated in our heads and it is these circuits that control our thoughts and movements. Indeed, the circuit is the movement because it dictates the content of each thought and the timing and strength of each muscle contraction.

More importantly, each time we practise something – be it a mental or physical skill – our nerve fibres are coated in a layer of insulating material called myelin which acts in much the same way as the rubber insulation that coats a copper wire: it makes the electrical impulses stronger and faster by preventing the signals from leaking out.

Each time we practise a skill, a new layer of myelin is added to the neurone and the thicker the myelin gets, the better it insulates our nerve fibres and, therefore, the faster our movements and thoughts become. But that's not all. As well as getting faster, our thoughts and movements also become more accurate as we add more and more layers of myelin. Why should this be? Because myelin regulates the velocity with which those electrical impulses travel through our nerve fibres, speeding up or slowing down the signals so that they hit our synapses at exactly the right moment. And timing is all important because neurones are binary: either they fire or they don't. Whether they fire is dependent on whether the incoming impulse is big enough to exceed their so-called "threshold of activation".

Neurochemistry teaches us, therefore, that every skill can be improved and perfected by performing it repeatedly because this helps us to hone our neural circuitry. But not all forms of practice are equal. We create myelin most effectively when we engage in deliberate practice

Deliberate practice is about struggling in certain targeted ways – placing artificial barriers in the way of our success in order to make it harder to learn something. In other words, you slow your learning down and force yourself to make mistakes. This is what Robert Bjork calls "desirable difficulties" and I will explore this concept in Chapter Eight on homework. For now, suffice to say, the act of slowing down and making mistakes ensures we are operating at the edges of our ability. So, the best form of practice – and therefore the best way to create more myelin – is to set yourself a target just beyond your current ability but within your reach. This is what Lev Vygotsky calls the "zone of proximal development" and what Robert Bjork calls "the sweet spot". This spot is the "optimal gap between what [we] know and what [we're] trying to do [and] when [we] find that sweet spot, learning takes off".

In the bonus chapter that follows Chapter Fourteen on the habits of academic success, I will explore what all the high-achieving pupils I've ever taught had in common. Having studied their methods and interviewed them, I have discovered that it is a case of cause and effect: it is precisely because these pupils attended school, were well-organised, completed work on time, and had an end goal in mind that they achieved excellent grades in their final exams. In short, the cause was diligent study and determination; the effect was high achievement.

In that chapter I will also argue that one way to emulate the success of my best pupils is to acquire a toolkit of effective study skills such as:

Self-quizzing - this is about retrieving knowledge and skills from memory and is far more effective than simply re-reading a text.

Elaboration - this is about relating new material to what pupils already know, explaining it to somebody else, or explaining how it relates to the wider world.

Generation - this is when pupils attempt to answer a question or solve a problem before being shown the answer or the solution.

Reflection - this involves taking a moment to review what has been learned by asking questions such as: What went well? What could have gone better? What other knowledge or experience does it remind me of? What strategies could I use next time to get better results?

Calibration - this is about removing the illusion of knowing and pupils actually answering all the questions or testing themselves on all the subject content even if they think they know the answers and that it is too easy.

Condition for learning #4: Feedback

In order to create the conditions for pupils to learn, we need to ensure they receive - and produce - information about what they have mastered and what they still need to practice.

Feedback should redirect the pupil's and the teacher's actions to help the pupil achieve their target. Effective feedback: addresses faulty interpretations; comments on rather than grades work; provides cues or prompts for further work; is timely, specific and clear; and is focused on task and process rather than on praising.

Feedback works best when it is explicit about the marking criteria, offers suggestions for improvement, and is focused on how pupils can close the gap between their current and their desired performance; it does not focus on presentation or quantity of work.

Feedback can promote the growth mindset if it: is as specific as possible; focuses on factors within pupils' control; focuses on factors which are dependent on effort not ability; and motivates rather than frustrates pupils.

Self- and peer-assessment can prove effective strategies - particularly as we want our pupils to become increasingly metacognitive in their approach to learning - because they: give pupils greater responsibility for their learning; allow pupils to help and be helped by each other; encourage collaboration and reflection; enable pupils to see their progress; and help pupils to see for themselves how to improve.

But self- and peer-assessment needs to be used wisely and pupils need to be helped to develop the necessary skills and knowledge because research suggests eighty per cent of the feedback pupils give each other is wrong. However, it is worth investing time in helping pupils to improve their self-assessment skills because research suggests it increases pupils' achievement.

Ultimately, though, the only useful feedback is that which is acted upon – it is crucial, therefore, that the teacher knows the pupil and knows when and what kind of feedback to give, then plans time for pupils to act on the feedback they receive. For example, DIRT - 'directed improvement and reflection time' - is a great use of lesson time at Key Stage 3 and helps to condition pupils in the drafting and re-drafting process, as well as gets them used to responding positively to feedback, to learning from their mistakes, and to improving through a process of trial and error.

Condition for learning #5: Metacognition

In order to create the conditions for pupils to learn, we need to ensure that they are afforded opportunities to explain key concepts to each other and learn by teaching, thereby taking ownership of their own and each other's learning. I've already written in some detail about metacognition and cooperative learning so shall not do so again here, except to share a few practical ideas for teaching metacognition.

Above, I explained that the most successful people in life have the capacity to self-monitor and self-adjust as needed; they proactively consider what is working, what isn't, and what might be done better. In order to prepare our pupils for Key Stage 4 and beyond, therefore, we need to engage them in some form of self-evaluation, teaching them how to take stock of what they have learned and what needs further inquiry or refinement.

In practice, this means that pupils need opportunities in lessons to self-monitor, self-assess, and self-adjust their work, individually and collectively, as the work progresses. We can do this by:

- Allocating five minutes in the middle and at the end of a lesson in order to consider 'What have we found out? What remains unresolved or unanswered?
- Asking pupils to attach a self-assessment form to every formal piece of work they hand in
- Including a one-minute essay at the end of an instruction-based lesson in which pupils summarise the two or three main points and the questions that still remain for them (and, thus, next time, for the teacher)
- Asking pupils to attach a note to any formal piece of work in which they are honest about what they do and do not understand
- Teaching pupils to evaluate work in the same way that teachers do so that pupils become more accurate as peer reviewers and self-assessors, and more inclined to "think like teachers" in their work.
- Starting lessons with a survey of the most burning questions pupils may have. Then, as part of the final

plenary, judge how well the questions were addressed, which ones remain, and what new ones emerged.

- Leaving the second half of a unit deliberately 'open' to allow pupils to frame and pursue the inquiry (rather than be directed by the teacher) based on the key questions that remain and clues that emerge at the end of the first half
- Getting pupils to develop a self-profile of their strengths and weaknesses as learners at the start of the year whereby they consider how they learn best, what strategies work well for them, what type of learning is most difficult, and what they wish to improve upon. Then, structure periodic opportunities for pupils to monitor their efforts and reflect on their struggles, and successes, and possible edits to their own profiles.

(This list is adapted from Teach 2: Educated Risks *by M J Bromley, Autus Books 2016)*

Condition for learning #6: Assessment

Finally, in order to create the conditions for pupils to learn, we need to involve them in making judgments about their own and others' achievements against the learning outcomes.

There's a whole chapter on assessment later in this book so I won't dedicate too much time to it here but I do want to explore a couple of methods of assessing pupils' understanding:

First, let's consider questioning...

Questioning

Questioning - and indeed all forms of classroom discussion - is a great way to assess pupils' understanding and, more importantly, of deepening that understanding.

Questions make pupils smarter because they make pupils think. Questions should only be used if they cause thinking and/or provide information for the teacher about what to do next. The best model of questioning is ABC whereby questions are passed around the classroom and pupils agree/disagree with, build upon, and challenge each other's responses. The Japanese call this neriage which means 'to polish' – pupils polish each other's answers, refining them, challenging each other's thinking.

It's a well-known fact by now that increasing 'wait time' – the amount of time the teacher waits for an answer to their question before either answering it themselves or asking someone else – makes pupils' answers longer, more confident, and increases pupils' ability to respond.

In open questions, the rubric defines the rigour. In multiple choice questions the options define the rigour. Effective assessment combines open and multiple-choice questions.

Second, let's look at constructive alignment...

Constructive alignment and the SOLO taxonomy

Constructive alignment is another great assessment tool. It's a concept that derives from cognitive psychology and constructivist theory and recognises the importance of linking new material to experiences in the learner's memory, as well as extrapolating that material to possible future contexts – connecting the learning, showing the bigger picture. The teacher makes a deliberate alignment between the planned learning activities and the learning outcomes. This is a conscious effort to provide the learner with a clearly defined goal, and a well-designed learning activity that is appropriate for the task. But, more importantly for our present purposes, it provides the pupil with well-designed assessment criteria for giving feedback once they've completed that task. In constructive alignment, the teacher starts with the outcomes they want pupils to learn, and then aligns teaching and assessment to those outcomes.

Constructive alignment marries well with the SOLO (structure of observed learning outcomes) taxonomy and helps to map levels of understanding that can be built into intended learning outcomes and create assessment criteria or rubrics.

SOLO consists of five levels of understanding:

1. *Pre-structural*: a pupil hasn't understood the point and offers a simple – incorrect – response;
2. *Uni-structural*: a pupil's response only focuses on one relevant aspect;
3. *Multi-structural*: here, a pupil's response focuses on several relevant aspects but these are treated independently of each other;
4. *Relational*: here, the different aspects seen at the multi-structural level have become integrated to form a coherent whole;
5. *Extended abstract*: the integrated whole is now conceptualised at a higher level of abstraction.

As pupils move up the five levels, their understanding grows from surface to deep to conceptual.

The SOLO taxonomy also helps develop a growth mindset because pupils come to understand that declarative and functioning learning outcomes are the result of effort and the use of effective strategies rather than the result of innate ability.

Once all six of these conditions for learning are in place, pupils will not only be able to learn but will be able to transfer their learning from one context to another - the measure of true learning.

To further support our pupils in developing this ability to 'transfer' their learning, we should also: Allow a sufficient amount of time for initial learning to take place; plan for distributed – or spaced – learning and engage in deliberate practice; make sure pupils are motivated to learn by planning work with sufficient challenge; teach information in multiple, contrasting contexts and/or in abstract form; teach metacognition so that pupils become expert at monitoring and regulating their learning.

The five keys to lesson planning

Now that we've established and defined the six conditions for learning, let's look at how we might incorporate these into our planning...

Lessons which meet the six conditions for learning which I outline above possess five common elements of design - what we might call a 'design for learning' or the 'five keys to lesson planning':

Firstly, lessons that meet the six conditions for learning make explicit the big picture. They do this by connecting the learning in three ways: 1. They articulate a clear learning goal that pupils understand - in other words, pupils are told where the lesson is headed. 2. They articulate a clear purpose for the learning - in other words, pupils are told why the learning goal is important and why they are learning what they're learning. 3. They ensure that pupils' starting points (what they already know as well as their misconceptions) are identified through pre-tests.

Secondly, lessons that meet the six conditions for learning ensure that subject content is tailored to meet individual needs and to match individual skills, interests, and styles. We do this by personalising the learning, by using diagnostic data about pupils' starting points and misconceptions (both that gathered from pre-tests and that gleaned from ongoing formative assessments in class) in order to inform the lesson planning process.

Thirdly, lessons that meet the six conditions for learning ensure that the learning activities pique and maintain pupils' interest by grabbing their attention from the very beginning. They do this by using sensory 'hooks' and by ensuring that the lesson is appropriately paced, and that subject content is appropriately varied and challenging.

Fourthly, lessons that meet the six conditions for learning ensure that pupils acquire the necessary experiences, knowledge and skills to meet the learning goals but in so doing they remember that less is more: they cover a smaller amount of curriculum content so that they can explore each concept in greater depth and detail - and from a range of different perspectives - than they would be able to achieve if they attempted to 'get through' more content.

Finally, lessons that meet the six conditions for learning provide pupils with regular opportunities to reflect on their progress, to revise their thinking and to re-draft their work, acting on the formative feedback they receive from teacher-, peer- and self-assessments.

And those are the five keys to lesson planning that will unlock the six conditions for learning I outlined earlier.

Here are a few other tips for planning Key Stage 3 lessons with which to conclude this section on the curriculum:

- When planning lessons, we should focus on what pupils will be made to think about rather than on what they will do. We might, for example, organise a lesson around a big question.

- We need to repeat learning several times – at least three times, in fact – if it is to penetrate pupils' long-term memories.
- Tests interrupt forgetting and reveal what has actually been learnt as well as what gaps exist. Accordingly, we should run pre-tests at the start of every unit – perhaps as a multiple-choice quiz – which will provide cues and improve subsequent learning. Retrieval activities like this also help pupils prepare for exams.
- We should plan lessons so that the information we teach 'sticks' in pupils' memories. We can do this by:
- ensuring that each lesson clearly articulates and is built around a simple idea – i.e. being clear about the key take-away message from each lesson, which could be a question or hypothesis.
- using metaphor to relate new ideas to prior knowledge and to create images in pupils' minds.

- piquing pupils' curiosity before we fill gaps in pupils' knowledge (thus convincing pupils they need the information we're about to give them access to). This can be done by asking pupils to make predictions or by setting a hypothesis to be proven or disproven.
- making abstract ideas concrete by grounding them in sensory reality (i.e. making pupils feel something). The richer – sensorily and emotionally – new information is, the more strongly it is encoded in pupils' memories.
- making ideas credible - showing rather than telling pupils something (e.g. experiments, field studies, etc. beat textbooks for 'stickability').

BONUS CHAPTER
Project-based learning

We know from Ron Berger's book An Ethic of Excellence that the first step towards encouraging pupils to produce high-quality work is to set assessment tasks which inspire and challenge them and which are predicated on the idea that every pupil will succeed, not just finish the task but produce work which represents personal excellence. We also know that the most effective assessment tasks offer pupils an opportunity to engage in genuine research not just research invented for the classroom. We know, too, that a pupil's finished product needs a real audience and that the role of the teacher is to help pupils to get their work ready for the public eye. This means there is a genuine reason to do the work well, not just because the teacher wants it that way. Not every piece of work can be of genuine importance, of course, but every piece of work can be displayed, presented, appreciated, and judged.

We know that assessment tasks work best when they are structured in such a way as to make it difficult for pupils to fall too far behind or fail. Tasks also work best when they are broken into a set of clear components so that pupils must progress through checkpoints to ensure they are keeping up. Good tasks have in-built flexibility to allow for a range of abilities. We also know that assessment tasks work best when they have in-built rubrics, checklists if you like, which make clear what is expected of each pupil at each stage of development. In other words, the rubric spells out exactly what components are required in the assignment, what the timeline for completion is, and on what qualities and dimensions the work will be judged.

However, we know it is not enough simply to make a list, a rubric, of what makes a good finished product, be that an essay or a science experiment. It is not enough to read a great piece of literature and analyse the writing, or to look at the work of a great scientist. If we want our pupils to write a strong essay, to design a strong experiment, we need to show them what a great essay or experiment looks like. We need to admire models, find inspiration in them, and analyse their strengths and weaknesses. In short, we need to work out what makes them strong. And what is the best way of achieving all the above and, therefore, one means of delivering the five principles of well-planned lessons we explored in the previous chapter? According to Berger - and many others besides - the answer is project-based learning.

When I think back to my own school days, the most lasting and colourful memories I have - well, the second most lasting and colourful memories I have (because what happens behind the bike sheds stays behind the bike sheds) - are of project work. I recall the excitement of being given a brief and knowing that I had the freedom to meet that brief in any way I wanted, to work independently over the course of several lessons, gathering evidence and testing a hypothesis or answering a big question, then presenting my findings in a creative and personal way. Many of us, when asked about a positive memory of school, will similarly remember a research project with real-world application that engaged us and that we were able to share with our friends and family.

According to the Galileo Educational Network (2004) - which designs and delivers enquiry-based learning in some American schools - project-based learning is "a dynamic process of being open to wonder and puzzlements and coming to know and understand the world". They go on to say that project-based learning is "a process whereby pupils are actively involved in their learning, formulate questions, investigate far and wide, and build understandings, meanings and knowledge [that is] new to pupils and may be used to answer a question, to develop a solution or to support a position or point of view."

Research, such as that carried out by Kuhne in 1995, suggests that using project-based learning with pupils can help them to become more creative, more positive and more independent. It helps if project-based learning forms part of the whole school culture, if it is common practice across all classes and year groups, and if it is the accepted mode of learning.

In order for schools to make project-based learning a part of their culture, senior leaders must have a clearly articulated vision for developing it and they must be strong in dedicating time and money to it, even despite competing pressures. In its early stages, there needs to be a group of enthusiastic champions willing to try it out and promote the advantages. Teachers need to collaborate and support each other. Problem-solving and investigative skills also need to be valued throughout the school.

But, whilst a whole school commitment to project-based learning is desirable, it is by no means essential... individual teachers can make it work in beautiful isolation in their own classrooms... According to Drayton and Falk (2002), individual classrooms in which teachers emphasise project-based learning - even when the rest of the school does not - tend to have the following characteristics:

- Projects take the form of real-life problems and work within the context of the curriculum and/or local community.
- Projects capitalise on the areas of pupils' natural curiosity.
- Data and information are actively used, interpreted, refined, digested and discussed.
- Teachers, pupils and other key staff (including, say, the school librarian) work together to plan projects.

- The local community relates to the project in some way, either as research material or audience, or indeed both.
- The teacher continually models the behaviours required of the pupil-researchers.
- The teacher uses the language required of the pupil-researchers on an ongoing basis.
- Pupils take ownership of their own learning from beginning to end.
- The teacher facilitates the process of gathering and presenting information.
- The teacher and pupils use technology to advance their project, both in information gathering and presenting.
- The teacher embraces project-based learning as both curriculum content and pedagogy.
- The teacher and pupils interact more frequently and more actively than during traditional instruction.

Building a culture of project-based learning in your classroom also means recognising, supporting and teaching the role of metacognition. Certainly, project-based learning provides opportunities for pupils to develop life skills (as explained by Hacker (1999) and Huhlthau (1988) among others) such as character or grit.

There are three strands of project-based learning well worth remembering - indeed, in many ways, these three are the cornerstones of effective projects:

1. A genuine outcome
2. Multiple drafts
3. Ongoing assessment

1. A genuine outcome

If pupils are to commit time and effort to their project, they need to know that there is a genuine outcome, a real audience and means of exhibition for their work. In other words, if pupils know their work is going to be put on public display, there to be critiqued by members of the public, including their family and friends and not just their teachers, they are more likely to work hard and produce their best quality work.

2. Multiple drafts

In real life, when the quality of work matters, we rarely submit our first attempt at something. By the time this book is published, for example, I will have drafted and redrafted it several times (so just imagine how bad my first draft must have been!) But in many schools pupils hand in their first attempt at something, have it marked and returned, then discard it before moving on to the next task.

Project-based learning enables pupils to positively engage with the drafting and redrafting process, and encourages them to make time for and recognise the importance of polishing work until such a time as it represents their very best efforts. Producing multiple drafts is not only a great way of teaching pupils about the real-life importance of redrafting, but it also provides great opportunities for personalised assessment... talking of which...

3. Ongoing assessment

Producing multiple drafts helps pupils to engage in formative assessment, learning from feedback and making gradual improvements. Re-drafting also enables pupils to learn from each other by critiquing each other's work. Regarded in this way, critique, - far from being a distraction or added burden - becomes integral to the learning process. Critique can become a lesson in its own right, providing opportunities for the teacher to give instruction, to introduce or refine concepts and skills. Such lessons can also bring pupils' misunderstandings to the fore, enabling the class to respond en masse.

Ron Berger argues that effective feedback is kind, specific and helpful. This is also a good way to structure critique sessions:

Kind: Presenting their work for critique puts pupils in a vulnerable position. The person critiquing work, on the other hand, can - in their enthusiasm and eagerness to help - say hurtful things, albeit inadvertently. Therefore, pupils need to be taught how to be kind and avoid personal attacks.

Specific: Although it is important to be kind, feedback must not - as a result - become too vague and anodyne; it must offer specific advice about how to improve if it is to be useful.

Helpful: Critique should not just be about articulating what is strong and what is not; it should also be about working out how to make the work even better; it should offer suggestions and ideas.

There are two main types of critique session: instructional critique and peer critique.

1. An instructional critique session is led by the teacher and usually involves the entire class. It can be used to introduce a model at the start of a project.

2. A peer critique session is what pupils use in order to get feedback on their drafts. Peer critique sessions are usually carried out in pairs or small groups, though they can also be carried out by a full class.

They might take the form of 'gallery' critique whereby work is displayed on the walls around the classroom and the class walks around the room taking notes on the drafts and sticking post-it notes to them offering general impressions and suggestions.

They might take the form of 'dilemma' critique whereby pupils are placed in groups of four or five and share something they're struggling with on their product, or share a draft, and then allow their fellow pupils to discuss possible solutions.

They might take the form of 'workshop' critique whereby pupils are placed in groups of three with specific teacher-generated questions about the product in hand. Pupils take turns presenting their product to the other two pupils and then discuss the questions as a way to improve the product's quality. Each pupil spends about 10–15 minutes on presenting and receiving feedback/critique.

Finally, they might take the form of 'pair' critique whereby two pupils work together to provide deeper critique, really digging into a product, evaluating the work, and challenging each other for 15–20 minutes.

Project-based learning also works best when pupils regard the project as personally meaningful and when it fulfils an educational purpose - in other words, when it is an integral part of the curriculum.

Ensuring a project is meaningful

A project can be made personally meaningful if we begin by triggering pupils' curiosity. In other words, at the start of the first lesson on the project, we use a 'hook' to engage our pupils' interest and initiate questioning. A hook can be anything: a video, a lively discussion, a guest speaker, a field trip, or a text. Many pupils find schoolwork meaningless because they don't perceive a need to know what they're being taught. They are not motivated by their teacher's insistence that they should learn something because they'll need it later in life or for the next module on the course, or because it might be in the exam. With a compelling project, however, the reason for the learning becomes clear: pupils need to know this in order to meet the challenge they've just accepted.

A project can also be made personally meaningful to pupils if we pose a big question which captures the heart of the project in clear, compelling language, and which gives pupils a sense of purpose and challenge. A big question should be provocative, open, and complex. The question can be abstract or concrete; or it can be focused on solving a problem. Without a big question, pupils may not understand why they are undertaking a project. They may know that the series of activities they are engaged in are in some way connected but may not be clear as to how or why. The big question is the string that binds the project together.

A project can be made personally meaningful to pupils if they are given some choice about how to conduct the project and present their findings. Indeed, the more choice, the better. Where choice is limited, pupils can select what topic to study within a general big question or choose how to design, create, and present their findings. In the middle of the choice spectrum, we might provide a small menu of options for creative final 'products' in order to prevent pupils from becoming overwhelmed by too many choices. Where choice is broad, pupils can decide what 'products' they will create, what resources they will use, and how they will use their time. Pupils might also choose their project's topic and big question.

Ensuring a project fulfils an educational purpose

A project can fulfil an educational purpose if it provides opportunities to build metacognition and character skills such as collaboration, communication, and critical thinking, which will serve pupils well in the workplace as in life.

A project can also fulfil an educational purpose if pupils conduct a real-life inquiry, rather than finding information in textbooks or on the Internet then making a poster. In projects with real-life application, pupils follow a trail that begins with their own questions, leads to a search for resources and the discovery of answers, and often ultimately leads to generating new questions, testing ideas, and drawing their own conclusions. With real-life projects comes innovation—a new answer to a big question, a new product, or an individually generated solution to a problem.

A project can also fulfil an educational purpose if it makes learning meaningful by emphasising the need to create high-quality products and performances through the formal use of feedback and drafting. As part of project-based learning, pupils learn that most people's first attempts don't result in high quality. Instead, frequent revision is a feature of real-world work. In addition to providing direct feedback, we can coach pupils in using rubrics and other sets of assessment criteria in order for pupils to critique each other's work.

Finally, a project can fulfil an educational purpose if it ends with a product being presented to a real audience. Work is more meaningful when it is produced not only for the teacher or the test but for a real public audience. This makes pupils care more about the quality of their work.

Let's look at how to plan, run and assess a project...

Planning a project

When planning a project, it is crucial that the topic is worthy of pupils' time and effort and will retain their interest over the medium-term. It is also important that it deliver sufficient curriculum content to be worthy of its timetabled commitment.

When selecting a topic, we should begin with the syllabus's programmes of study and select an area that will intrigue and interest pupils. The next step is to set out objectives for the project and to plan the activities. We should choose a curriculum-based theme for which background knowledge will already have been developed prior to the project starting because pupils will need to bring a strong background of experience and knowledge with them. We should consider whether the theme presents sufficient opportunities to engage all pupils in the class, including males and females, the highly motivated as well as those who require a lot of encouragement, and the more able as well as those who require more support and scaffolding.

If using project-based learning for the first time, we should try to limit the scope of the project in terms of time, topic and end-product, and focus on ensuring the success of all pupils. We should consider how many product formats we are willing to teach and make sure that pupils share information in a way that is very simple or very familiar to them.

Running a project

As well as a means of delivering the curriculum, projects help pupils to acquire and develop research and employability skills. This works best when project-based learning is integrated within the curriculum, is taught with a focus on developing critical thinkers, is made relevant to pupils' lives and needs, and is related to their past experiences.

As pupils work through the project, we teachers - by employing a personalised approach - need to help our pupils to locate, analyse and use the information they find. We need to assist them to clarify their thinking through questioning, paraphrasing and talking through tasks. We need to provide them with opportunities to record information, and we need to evaluate their progress.

Broadly speaking, there are five main phases to a project:

Phase 1: Piquing curiosity and agreeing key questions for investigation

Project-based learning begins by piquing pupils' interest in or curiosity about a topic. It is a big question that begs an answer, a hypothesis that demands to be proven or disproven, a puzzle that simply must be solved.

For those pupils with little or no background knowledge of a topic, we need to provide information and contextual knowledge in order to motivate pupils. Once pupils are interested and engaged in a general topic or theme, they need to be involved in determining what particular questions will be investigated, how they might find the information they need about a topic, how to present information to a particular audience, and what criteria for evaluating their research product and process might best be used.

Phase 2: Assimilating existing knowledge and gathering new evidence

Next, pupils need to think about the information they already have on the topic and agree the information they need to find and how best to gather that information. Pupils may need to spend a considerable amount of time exploring and analysing the information they have and they gather in order to determine their key focus for the project.

We will often need to help pupils understand that the information they find, whether in a book, a newspaper or on the internet, was created by people with particular beliefs and purposes and that, therefore, the information is likely to be subjective rather than objective. As such, it's important that we teach pupils to be able to identify emotive language and bias.

Phase 3: Finding a focus

Next, pupils will find a focus for their project. A focus is the aspect of a topic that, armed with all the information they need, the pupil decides to investigate. Coming to a focus can be very difficult for pupils because it involves more than just narrowing the scope of the topic. It also involves agreeing a big question or hypothesis, perhaps offering a personal perspective, too.

Phase 4: Organising and sharing information

Pupils then need to organise the information they've gathered, putting the information into their own words and creating a presentation - using their preferred format perhaps.

Once the presentation is ready, it should be shared, ideally with a real audience outside the classroom.

Teaching pupils audience appreciation skills and strategies, focusing on the positive, helps to support pupils through this phase.

Phase 5: Evaluating the project

Finally, when a research project is complete, pupils need to understand and question the assessment criteria, to identify the various steps in their project process, and to share their feelings about that process. Pupils should be able to articulate the importance of this work in terms of how it has helped them develop their metacognitive skills, and they should be able to see connections between their project work in school and work or activities that they have completed outside of school.

Assessing a project

When designing projects, we need to plan for ongoing assessments and these assessments should take three forms: diagnostic, formative and summative.

1. Diagnostic assessment is used to find out which metacognitive skills and strategies pupils already know and can use at the start of a project which can then be built on during the project. Areas of weakness and difficulty can also be targeted at this stage to help plan direct instruction during the project. Diagnostic assessments also help us to recognise when personalised or differentiated instruction may be necessary for certain pupils in a class.

2. Formative assessment is critical in the planning of project-based learning activities. Ongoing formative assessment helps us to identify the development of our pupils' skills and strategies and to monitor pupils' planning, retrieving, processing and creating skills during research activity. This ongoing assessment allows us to modify instruction, adapt the project activity and support pupils with special instructional needs.

3. Summative assessment is carried out at the end of the project in order to provide information to pupils, parents and teachers about pupils' progress and achievement on the project. This type of assessment helps us and our pupils to plan for further projects. Summative assessment assesses both the content and the process of the project.

Project assessments should involve pupils in identifying and/or creating the criteria used to evaluate pupil work and this criterion should be communicated before pupils begin tasks so that they can plan for success and so that they understand what is expected of them.

Project assessments should form part of an ongoing process rather than be regarded as an isolated event, and should focus on both process and product. Assessments should also provide opportunities for pupils to revise their work, enabling them to set goals and improve their learning by providing a status report on how well pupils can demonstrate their learning and progress at any one time. Assessment feedback should be developmentally appropriate, age-appropriate, and should consider pupils' cultural and individual needs. Assessment data should consider multiple sources of evidence (including both formal and informal), and provide opportunities for pupils to demonstrate what they know, understand and can do.

To conclude this chapter on project-based learning, here is a useful flowchart summarising the process:

1. Pupils select a topic to research within the parameters set by the teacher.
2. Pupils develop and support a position or point of view, this may be a big question that needs answering or a hypothesis that needs proving or disproving.
3. Pupils relate their existing knowledge and understanding of their topic and identify any gaps and areas that require further study.
4. Pupils conduct research to develop an in-depth understanding. This may include using textbooks, the Internet, and conducting interviews. Pupils are taught the relevant research skills as well as codes of ethics and confidentiality as appropriate.
5. Pupils record information using the most appropriate note-taking strategies.
6. Pupils carefully select and evaluate key information from a variety of sources.
7. Pupils create a report or presentation based on guidelines developed in the planning phase and in response to the needs and interests of the intended audience.
8. Pupils use technology as appropriate in order to enhance their presentations and reports.

9. Pupils share their final report/project with larger groups, with other classes, in the community and/or with family.
10. The teacher identifies and shares the evaluation criteria for the process and the product.
11. Pupils are involved in setting evaluation criteria for the process and the product.
12. Pupils provide appropriate self-evaluation and peer evaluation of the final product and the inquiry process.
13. Pupils monitor and adapt their own inquiry skills and strategies during the process.
14. Pupils share their feelings and progress each lesson.
15. Teacher monitors progress at the end of each lesson.
16. Pupils talk about what went well and what was challenging.

Part Four

Making Homework Count

CHAPTER THIRTEEN
What homework works best?

Before we consider what homework works best and how much of it to set, we need to tackle the elephant in the room: What's the point of homework? I ask this question because, it seems to me, that homework has had a rough ride in recent years with many teachers and parents calling for it to be scrapped completely. Those who fail to see the merits of homework tend to cite John Hattie's book 'Visible Learning' which gives homework an effect size of 0.26, meaning there's only a 21% chance that homework will make a positive difference to a pupil's levels of progress.

One prominent advocate of scrapping homework is Tim Lott of The Guardian who, in October 2012, admitted to "a profound dislike of homework" and asked "Why do we torment kids in this way?" He went on to say:

"I had no homework during my primary school years and very little during the first years of grammar school. This was the norm in the 1960s and 70s. At some point since, the work "ethic" that has infected national life generally – not that it's particularly ethical – insists that if you're not working, you're doing something faintly dissolute or purposeless, even if you're six.

"Nothing is more precious than those islands of childhood that are left untouched by invading adults and their fund of schemes for the future when you finally make it as a "worthy citizen". Let children drift and dream and make up games with plastic guns and My Little Pony, watch unsuitable TV and stare out the window. But this makes evangelists for the work society uneasy."

Lott, in turn, cites Sara Bennet and Nancy Kalish who - in their book 'The Case Against Homework' point out that "all the credible research on homework suggests that for younger kids, homework has no connection with positive learning outcomes and for older kids, the benefits of homework level off sharply after the first couple of assignments."

Homework generates conflict with parents, Lott says, and, worse still, parents are required to help. The problem is, most parents are not trained teachers and are often impatient and ineffective. The result of homework, according to Lott and many others, is that study becomes associated in the young mind with conflict and unhappiness.

But the facts are a little more nuanced. It's probably true that too much homework - particularly if it's meaningless 'fluff' - for Lott's 10-year-old daughter is pointless, counterproductive and switches her and her parents off education. But that's not the whole story. The benefits of homework vary by age; the older the pupil, the greater the benefit. Indeed, if you look in detail at what Hattie says in 'Visible Learning', you'll see that behind the headline figure of 0.26 are two separate figures, one for primary and one for secondary and those two figures are startlingly different.

But first let's look at effect sizes in general. An effect size of 0.2 is considered small. An effect size of 0.4 is considered medium. An effect size of 0.6 is considered large. Anything greater than 0.4 is therefore above average and anything above 0.6 is classed as excellent.

Hattie says that the effect of homework on pupil outcomes is 0.26 overall but is 0.15 at primary and 0.64 at secondary. Therefore, it is small at primary but large at secondary. In other words, the effect of homework on pupil outcomes in the primary phase is, as Lott and others rightly argue, negligible and could do more harm than good if it's not managed well. But the effect of homework on pupil outcomes in the secondary phase of education is excellent and therefore well worth persevering with, albeit improving.

Homework, then, is not to be disregarded quite so quickly... But what kind of homework works best at Key Stage 3 and how much homework should we set pupils in Years 7, 8 and 9?

What homework works best?

In Visible Learning, Hattie goes into some detail about the kinds of homework that work best. The highest effects, he says, are associated with practice and rehearsal tasks. And short, frequent homework tasks which are closely monitored by the teacher have the most impact on pupil progress.

The optimal time per night for pupils to spend on homework also varies by age; the older the pupil, the more time they should spend on homework. This is an imperfect science but, roughly, I would argue that the following is a good guide: pupils in the primary phase should do no more than about 20 minutes' homework a night, pupils in Key Stage 3 should do about 40 minutes, pupils in Key Stage 4 should do about 60 minutes, and pupils in Key Stage 5 (post-16) should do about 90 minutes a night.

In my experience, homework - like all forms of assignment - works best when you give pupils a clear picture of the final product and a real audience for their work. Homework also works best when you allow a certain degree of autonomy, whereby pupils can make choices about which tasks they carry out, how they carry them out and how they will be assessed on the final product. And homework also works best when you incorporate cultural products into it such as TV, film, magazines, food, and sports - to name but five examples - in order to engage pupils' personal interests and awaken prior knowledge.

Naturally, it is always best to avoid 'fluff' assignments - homework tasks which bear no relation to what is being learnt and which simply waste pupils' time. My daughter recently baked a cake in the shape of a wind turbine for a science project. It took her five hours. Needless to say, I was less than impressed. What aspect of science did she practice, rehearse or consolidate during those five hours, I asked her. She struggled for an answer. 'But I like baking,' came her eventual reply. Homework must have genuine purpose and the 'doing' must be linked to the 'learning' because pupils remember what they are asked to do more than what they are asked to think about.

It is also wise to try vary the language of homework tasks, perhaps by using Bloom's taxonomy. Rather than always asking pupils simple comprehension questions or to summarise a text, try to move up and down the taxonomy by asking them to: define, recall, describe, label, identify, match, name, or state (knowledge); translate, predict, explain, summarise, describe, compare, or classify (comprehension); demonstrate how, solve, use, interpret, relate, or apply (application); analyse, explain, infer, break down, prioritise, reason logically, or draw conclusions (analysis); design, create, compose, combine, reorganise, reflect, predict, speculate, hypothesise, or summarise (synthesis); assess, judge, compare/contrast, or evaluate (evaluation).

Homework, if it is to be taken seriously, should be non-negotiable like class-work. As such, you should not allow 'passes' whereby pupils can be excused from handing homework in and you should require everyone to 'turn in a paper' so even when someone has forgotten to bring their homework in to school on the due-date they should be required to write their name on a piece of paper and the reason they haven't got their homework and submit that instead. Then, crucially, at the bottom of the page they should add their parent's name and daytime phone number. That way you have a paper from everyone, a record of who hasn't handed their homework in on time and a way of contacting parents to make them aware of their child's failure to comply with the rules. I'm sure you'll find the tactic of requiring pupils to submit their parents' phone numbers will quickly have the desired effect.

Occasionally, homework could be integrated with other subjects, becoming cross-curricular and thematic, enabling pupils to see the natural links that exist between subjects and the transferability of key skills, as well as to provide variety. This could occur once every half term as an extended project.

Types of homework

Broadly speaking there are four types of homework task:

1. Practice
2. Preparation
3. Study
4. Extend or elaborate

Of these, practice is the most valuable in terms of producing measurable academic gains because practice builds proficiency and mastery. Practice can be single skill or cumulative. Cumulative practice is where a new skill is practised alongside a previously-learnt skill. A pupil must have demonstrated competence in the skill being practised before being asked to do it for homework. Homework should not - except in the case of flipped learning, which we will discuss in a moment - introduce new concepts or information.

There are three forms of practice worth considering for homework tasks:

1. Spaced repetition. This is where information is learnt initially then repeated several times at increasingly long intervals so that pupils get to the point of almost forgetting what they've learnt and must delve into their long-term memories to retrieve their prior

knowledge, thus strengthening those memories. This is because a memory is a neural connection and thoughts and experiences build connections between the billions of neurones in our brains, establishing new networks and patterns. Neural connections fade away if they are neglected but can get stronger with repeated use because repetition leads to neural habits of thought. In other words, the more often we repeat learning, the better the information will be learnt. But that's not all. As well as returning to prior learning following an interval, we should explore that information in a new way because making new associations further strengthens our memories, hence homework task number two...

2. Retrieval practice. This is testing or quizzing (such as multiple choice) used not for the purposes of assessment but for reinforcement and to provide pupils with feedback information on what they know and don't yet know so that they can better focus their future studies. As I explained above, a memory is a neural connection which fades away if it is neglected but can get stronger with repeated use. The more often we repeat learning, the better the information is learnt. As well as returning to prior learning following an interval, we should explore that information in a new way because making new associations further strengthens our memories.

The number of different connections we make influences the number of times memories are revisited, which in turn influences the length of time we retain a memory. When we connect different pieces of information with each other, we retain them for longer, because we retrieve them more often. It follows, then, that the more often we connect what we are teaching today to what we taught previously, the better the information will be learnt. If we retrieve a memory in order to connect prior knowledge to new information, the memory is strengthened even further so using quizzes in which the information is presented in new ways helps pupils to improve their learning. We could also plan opportunities for our pupils to reorganise the information they've learnt by writing about it or talking about it.

3. Cognitive disfluency (otherwise known as desirable difficulties). This is a memory technique that makes learning stick by placing artificial barriers in the way of pupils' learning. Doing this means that the process of encoding (initial learning) is made harder so that the process of retrieval (recalling that learning later, say in a test) is made easier. One example of a desirable difficulty is making learning materials less easy to read, perhaps by using a difficult to decipher font, in order to make pupils think harder about the content. Another example is to use more complex language when forming questions and tasks so that pupils must think harder about what is being asked of them before tackling the work.

Before we move on to flipped learning, let's conclude with some general homework do's and don'ts:

Don't:
- Use a one size fits all approach - homework should be differentiated to meet individual pupil needs
- Set homework that contains new information - it should be used to practice taught skills
- Set homework too quickly at the end of a lesson - time needs to be spent explaining it
- Collect homework in but not review it - it needs to be assessed and feedback given
- Give out homework that has no purpose or objective

Do:
- Give less homework but more often
- Have a specific purpose for every homework task you set; don't set 'busy work'
- Ensure that homework is engaging

- Allot sufficient time in the lesson to present and explain the homework
- Answer pupils' questions about the homework and check their understanding
- Articulate the rationale for the homework and how it will be assessed
- Provide timely feedback on what has been mastered and what still needs to be practised
- Provide choices about the homework task, format and presentation

Flipped learning

One increasingly popular form of homework - and indeed learning in general - is flipped learning.

Flipped learning, as the name suggests, 'flips' on its head the traditional idea of the classroom being used for lectures and the home being used for answering questions about that lecture.

Flipped learning effectively redefines homework because assignments involve video lectures which are viewed at home (or during private study time in school for pupils who don't have Internet access at home) as many times as pupils wish in order to digest difficult concepts. Class time is then freed up for pupils to ask questions and participate in collaborative work.

Flipped learning changes the distribution of teacher time. In a traditional classroom, the teacher tends to engage more with those pupils who ask questions rather than those who do not. But it is those who do not who invariably need the most help. Flipped learning ensures that the teacher's time is more fairly distributed.

When flipped learning is used, it is important that learning materials are varied rather than relying solely on video lectures which can quickly become repetitive and switch pupils off. Instead, teachers can use audio files and reading materials as well as video, and can source these from a variety of organisations including the Khan Academy and TED.

It is important, as with any task that relies on the use of technology, that there is fair access in school and that sufficient time is allowed between a homework being set and then being collected for pupils to access the materials.

Finally, the shorter the videos, audio files or reading materials, (3-6 minutes is ideal), the more likely it is that pupils will engage with the material and watch, listen or read them more than once, thus strengthening their learning. If the material is short, more flipped learning tasks can be set, too, in order to move the classroom learning forwards at a more rapid pace.

CHAPTER FOURTEEN
Engaging parents

In Part One of this book I said that the social and personal transition 'bridge' is concerned with forging links between a school and its pupils and their parents prior to and immediately after transfer. I went on to say that, in order to make a success of transition, feeder primary schools should operate an open-door policy for parents to air any concerns and questions whilst secondary schools should hold parents' evenings in the summer and autumn terms. But what more can be done to ensure that the communication between schools and parents is effective and why does this matter...?

A MetLife survey in 2005 said that the biggest challenge faced by new teachers was engaging with and involving parents. MetLife research from 2012 suggests that, although home-school communications have improved over the last twenty-five years or so, parental engagement continues to be an area of improvement for most schools.

And yet parental engagement is of great import in all sorts of ways. For example, according to Butler et el (2008), Haynes et al (1989), and Henderson (1987), it is associated with higher academic achievement. Butler et el (2008) and Haynes et al (1989) also claim that effective parental engagement leads to increased rates of pupil attendance whilst Becher (1984) and Henderson et al (1986) say it can have a positive effect on students' attitudes to learning as well as on their behaviour. Research has also shown that getting communication with parents right can lead to an increased level of interest in pupils' work (see, for example, Rich [1988] and Tobolka [2006]), increased parent satisfaction with their child's teachers (see Rich [1988]), and higher rates of teacher satisfaction (see MetLife [2012]).

So, the big question now is how can we improve parental engagement at Key Stage 3 and, in particular, with regards the transition process?

Firstly, communication needs to start early and continue throughout the transition process. The parents of pupils moving from Year 6 to Year 7 will not want to receive information halfway through the summer holidays at which point it will be deemed too late. Schools need to engage with parents early and clearly set out their expectations and requirements.

Secondly, communication needs to be a two-way process: as well as the school staying in touch with parents, parents also need a means of keeping in contact with the school throughout the transition process. One way to do this is to create an FAQ page, as well as a Q&A facility and a forum on the school's website.

Thirdly, one way to ensure communications are appropriately timed, relevant and useful is to utilise the experience and expertise of current Year 7 pupils and their parents. For example, the parents of current Year 7 pupils will be able to share their thoughts on what information they needed when they went through the transition process with their child not so long ago, as well as when they needed it most, whilst current Year 7 pupils will be able to offer their advice about how to prepare for secondary school by, to give but two examples, providing a reading list for the summer and sharing their advice about how to get ready for the first day of school.

Fourthly, communication should take myriad forms and should embrace new and emerging technologies.

The use of technologies such as email, texting, websites, electronic portfolios and online assessment and reporting tools have - accordingly to Merkley, Schmidt, Dirksen and Fuhler (2006) - made communication between parents and teachers more timely, efficient, productive and satisfying.

So, what might technology used to communicate with parents look like in practice? Here are a few suggestions for how technology could be used to help you communicate with parents and, indeed, vice versa:

- Parents could send teachers an email to let them know when the home learning environment may be (temporarily or otherwise) holding a pupil back.
- Likewise, teachers could send parents an email to let them know when issues arise at school which may have a detrimental effect on the pupil, such as noticeable changes in behaviour or deficits in academic performance.
- Teachers could text parents at the end of the day on which a student has done something particularly well or shown real progress or promise. Instant and personal feedback like this is valuable and helps make a connection between the teacher and a child's parents.
- Teachers could send half-termly or monthly newsletters via email to parents to inform them about which topics they are covering in class in the coming weeks, what homework will be set and when, and how parents can help.
- The school could use text, email and the school website to keep parents updated on forthcoming field trips, parent association meetings and other school activities.
- Teachers could use email to send out regular tips to parents on how they might be able to support their child's learning that week/month. For example, they could send a list of questions to ask their child about what students have been learning in class. They could also send hyperlinks to interactive quizzes or games.

- The school could use the school website to gather more frequent and informal parent voice feedback about specific topics. For example, they might post a short survey after each open evening and parents' evening.
- The school could provide an online calendar via its website to allow parents to volunteer to help in class, say as reading mentors or helpers at special events.
- An online calendar could also be used as a booking facility to enable parents to make their own meetings with school staff rather than having to phone the school, which many people find daunting.
- The online calendar could prove useful for booking slots at parents' evenings and other open evenings and events, enabling parents to be in control of the times at which they attend school rather than relying on a child and their teachers to agree suitable slots.

How to engage 'hard-to-reach' parents

Even once a school has established and embedded an effective parental engagement strategy, some parents are likely to remain hard to reach and it's often these parents that a school needs to engage with the most.

So why do some parents find it difficult to talk to their child's school? Sometimes it's because they lead busy, complicated lives and schools don't often present themselves as being high on their to-do list. Also, school's operating hours tend to clash with parents' working lives. Other times, it's because a parent had a difficult experience of school as a youngster and remains reluctant to enter a school building or talk with teachers. They may be daunted and even afraid. In both these cases, a school may need to consider alternative approaches, such as engaging with parents by telephone in the evenings and weekends, or meeting with them at another - neutral - location nearby, perhaps even using a 'go-between' such as another parent who is known to be engaged and reliable.

Some parents may have poor levels of literacy and so will need to be communicated with more sensitively in order that they do not misunderstand the nature and purpose of the communication, and in order to make it easier for them to respond without fear of humiliation.

Hard-to-reach parents are often the parents that schools need to reach most because their children - as a result of a lack of involvement or interest at home - attend school infrequently or late, present behavioural challenges when they do attend, and/or have low levels of literacy and/or numeracy. Where parents have consistently condoned their child's absence from school, there is much to be done in establishing and developing positive relationships between the school and the parents, and in educating parents on the impact of poor attendance.

The appointment of a specialist, such as a home-school liaison officer, may prove a successful approach where schools need to improve achievement in the longer term.

Much depends on building up and sustaining positive relationships between parents and the school. The introduction of rewards and incentives (that are also seen as being attractive to pupils) can help promote improved attendance, behaviour and achievement. Parents will have their own views about such reward schemes and should be consulted.

Engaging recently-immigrated parents

Some parents are hard to reach because they are newly arrived in the UK, have nascent (or no) English skills, and feel alienated from society and schools. Moreover, language and cultural differences can make parents feel intimidated by schools. It's also possible that some parents emigrated from a country where parental involvement in their child's school was actively discouraged, and their re-education in the ways of English schooling may prove a significant barrier for them.

One solution to this challenge is to arrange for a mother-tongue speaker to meet with parents, offering classes in English language and/or offering induction sessions to help parents become more familiar with and confident in their understanding of the school system in the UK.

This works both ways, of course...

A school may also benefit from arranging information sessions run by recently-immigrated parents and aimed at helping school staff to gain a better understanding of the lifestyles, traditions and customs of local ethnic minority groups.

Improving parental engagement is not without its challenges, of course. Here are a few barriers you will need to consider and overcome if you are to increase the effectiveness of your communications with parents and, consequently, improve the transition process for pupils entering Key Stage 3:

1. Parents might perceive the school as presenting obstacles in the form of a lack of encouragement, not informing parents of what they can do, and having too little scope for fitting around busy working and family lives.

2. Parents might face numerous barriers to engagement, including costs, time and transportation, language (for some parents for whom English is not a first language), low levels of literacy and numeracy, and a lack of confidence in supporting children's learning or engaging with a school.

3. Sustainability might be an issue, retaining committed and inspiring senior leaders, high levels of commitment across staff teams, and access to the funding streams and resources that successful programmes require.

4. Reaching and involving parents who have chosen not to engage either with their children's school or with their children's learning might be a challenge.

5. Lack of staff experience and knowledge of working to support parents in engaging with their children's learning might be a barrier.

To conclude this chapter, I'll share the recommendations of a 2010 Department for Education review of best practice in parental engagement. The report recommended that schools develop a parental engagement strategy which contains the following key features:

1. Planning - parental engagement must be planned for and embedded in the whole school strategy. The planning cycle should include a comprehensive needs analysis; the establishment of mutual priorities; ongoing monitoring and evaluation of interventions; and a public awareness process to help parents and teachers understand and commit to a strategic plan.

2. Leadership - effective leadership of parental engagement is essential to the success of programmes and strategies. A parental engagement programme is often led by a senior leader, although leadership may also be distributed in the context of a programme or cluster of schools and services working to a clear strategic direction.

3. Collaboration and engagement - parental engagement requires active collaboration with parents and should be proactive rather than reactive. It should

be sensitive to the circumstances of all families, recognise the contributions parents can make, and aim to empower parents.

4. Sustained improvement - a parental engagement strategy should be the subject of ongoing support, monitoring and development. This will include strategic planning which embeds parental engagement in whole-school development plans, sustained support, resourcing and training, community involvement at all levels of management, and a continuous system of evidence based development and review.

BONUS CHAPTER
What are the habits of academic success?

I don't believe in conspiracy theories but Abraham Lincoln and John F Kennedy have always made my spine tingle. After all, they have an awful lot in common...

Abraham Lincoln was elected to Congress in 1846; John F. Kennedy was elected to Congress in 1946. Abraham Lincoln was elected president in 1860; John F Kennedy was elected president in 1960. The names Lincoln and Kennedy each contain seven letters. Both men were particularly concerned with civil rights. Both their wives lost children while living in the White House. Both presidents were shot on a Friday. Both were shot in the head. Lincoln's secretary, Kennedy, warned him not to go to the theatre; Kennedy's secretary, Lincoln, warned him not to go to Dallas. Both were assassinated by Southerners. Both were succeeded by Southerners. Both successors were named Johnson: Andrew Johnson, who succeeded Lincoln, was born in 1808; Lyndon Johnson, who succeeded Kennedy, was born in 1908. Both assassins were known by three names which comprised 15 letters: John Wilkes Booth was born in 1839; Lee Harvey Oswald was born in 1939. Having assassinated Lincoln, Booth ran from the theatre and was caught in a warehouse; having assassinated Kennedy, Oswald ran from a warehouse and was caught in a theatre. Both Booth and Oswald were assassinated before their trials.

Spooky, eh? I don't know about you, but the hairs on the back of my neck are standing up. But, as I say, I don't believe in conspiracy theories. I do, however, believe in coincidence. So, what's the difference? When you think about it, coincidences aren't spooky at all; they are, in fact, perfectly rational because they express a simple, logical pattern of cause and effect. Take, for example, academic achievement...

Several years ago, while working as a deputy headteacher, I interviewed fifty pupils in years 11 and 13 who had achieved high grades in their GCSE and A level exams. I found something spooky – a series of apparent coincidences. For example, ...

All the pupils I interviewed had an attendance of more than 93 per cent; 90 per cent of them had a perfect attendance record. All the pupils I interviewed told me they used their planners regularly and considered themselves to be well-organised. As a result, all the pupils I interviewed completed their homework on time and without fail. All the pupils I interviewed told me they always asked for help from their teachers when they got stuck. They didn't regard doing so as a sign of weakness, rather a sign of strength. Admitting they didn't know something and asking questions meant they learnt something new and increased their intelligence.

Most of the pupils I interviewed were involved in clubs, sports, or hobbies at lunchtime, after school and/or at weekends. Though not all were sporting, they did all have get-up-and-go attitudes. They didn't spend every evening and weekend watching television. They were sociable and, to unwind, they read books. Lots of books. In fact, the school library confirmed that my cohort of high-achievers were among the biggest borrowers in school. All the pupils believed that doing well in school would increase their chances of getting higher paid and more interesting jobs later in life.

Many of them had a clear idea about the kind of job they wanted to do and knew what was needed in order to get it. They had researched the entry requirements and had then mapped out the necessary school, college, and/or university paths. They had connected what they were doing in school with achieving their future ambitions. School work and good exam results had a purpose, they were means to an important end.

Was it spooky that nearly all these high-achieving pupils had done the same things? Or was it a simple case of cause and effect: because these pupils shared these traits they went on to succeed? I believe it was the latter: it was because these pupils had attended school, were well organised, completed work on time, and had an end goal in mind that they had achieved excellent grades in their final exams. The cause was diligent study and determination; the effect was high achievement. As such, these young people can teach our pupils a valuable lesson - that the recipe for success is to:

- Have good attendance and punctuality.
- Be organised and complete all work on time.
- Be willing to ask for help when you're stuck.
- Have something to aim for and be ambitious.
- Map out your career path and be determined to succeed.

I now wish to explore the second of these ingredients in more detail: personal organisation. One means of becoming better organised is to acquire effective study skills. According to Paul C Brown et al in Make It Stick, the following study skills are proven to be particularly helpful to pupils...

1. Self-quizzing

Self-quizzing is about retrieving knowledge and skills from memory and is far more effective than simply re-reading a text. When your pupils read a text or study notes, you should teach them to pause periodically to ask themselves questions – without looking in the text – such as:

- What are the key ideas?
- What terms or ideas are new to me? How would I define them?
- How do the ideas in this text relate to what I already know?

You should set aside a little time every week for your pupils to quiz themselves on the current week's work and the material you have covered in previous weeks. Once they have self-quizzed, get your pupils to check their answers and make sure they have an accurate understanding of what they know and what they don't know. Your pupils need to know that making mistakes will not set them back, so long as they check their answers later and correct any errors.

You should space out your pupils' retrieval practice. This means studying information more than once and leaving increasingly large gaps between practice sessions. Initially, new material should be revisited within a day or so then not again for several days or a week. When your pupils are feeling surer of certain material, they should quiz themselves on it once a month. They should also interleave the study of two or more topics so that alternating between them requires them to continually refresh their memories of each topic.

2. Elaboration

Elaboration is the process of finding additional layers of meaning in new material. It involves relating new material to what pupils already know, explaining it to somebody else, or explaining how it relates to the wider world. An effective form of elaboration is to use a metaphor or image for the new material.

3. Generation

Generation is when pupils attempt to answer a question or solve a problem before being shown the answer or the solution. The act of filling in a missing word (the cloze test) results in better learning and a stronger memory of the text than simply reading the text. Before reading new class material, ask pupils to explain the key ideas they expect to find and how they expect these ideas will relate to their prior knowledge.

4. Reflection

Reflection involves taking a moment to review what has been learned. Pupils ask questions such as:
- What went well? What could have gone better?
- What other knowledge or experience does it remind me of?
- What might I need to learn in order to achieve better mastery?
- What strategies could I use next time to get better results?

5. Calibration

Calibration is achieved when pupils adjust their judgment to reflect reality – in other words, they become certain that their sense of what they know and can do is accurate. Often when we revise information, we look at a question and convince ourselves that we know the answer, then move on to the next question without trying to answer the previous one. If we do not write down an answer, we may create the illusion of knowing when in fact we would have difficulty giving a response. We need to teach our pupils to remove the illusion of knowing and answer all the questions even if they think they know the answer and that it is too easy.

Here are some other useful study skills we could teach our pupils:

1. Anticipate test questions during lessons.
2. Read study guides, find terms they can't recall or don't know and learn them.
3. Copy key terms and their definitions into a notebook.
4. Take practice tests.
5. Reorganise class material into a study guide.
6. Copy out key concepts and regularly test themselves on them.

7.   Space out revision and practice activities.

And here are some handy tips to help our pupils to study smarter:

Create desirable difficulties in the classroom by using tests frequently. Design study tools that make use of retrieval practice, generation and elaboration.

Return to concepts covered earlier in the term. Space, interleave and vary the topics covered in class so that pupils frequently have to "reload" what they already know about each topic in order to determine how new material relates to, or indeed differs from, prior knowledge.

Make learning transparent by helping your pupils to understand the ways in which you have incorporated desirable difficulties and other strategies into your lessons.

Plan for "free recall", whereby pupils spend 10 minutes at the end of each lesson filling a blank piece of paper with everything they can remember from that lesson.

Set a weekly homework whereby pupils create summary sheets (perhaps a side of A4) on which they summarise the previous week's learning in text, annotated illustrations, or graphical organisers. The purpose of this task is to stimulate retrieval and reflection, and to capture the previous week's learning before it is lost.

And finally, explain how learning works. Help your pupils to understand that creating some kinds of difficulties during the learning process helps to strengthen learning and memory because when learning is easy it is often superficial and soon forgotten. Help your pupils to understand that not all intellectual abilities are innate – in fact, when learning is "effortful", it changes the brain, making new connections and increasing intellectual ability. Pupils learn better when they struggle with new problems by themselves before being shown the solution, not vice-versa. Help your pupils to understand that, in order to achieve excellence, they must strive to surpass their current level of ability. This, by its very nature, often leads to set-backs and set-backs are often what provide the information that's needed in order to achieve mastery.

Part Five

Making Data Count

CHAPTER FIFTEEN
Diminishing the difference

One in four children in the UK grows up in poverty. The attainment gap between rich and poor is detectable at an early age (22 months) and widens throughout the education system. Children from the lowest income homes are half as likely to get five good GCSEs and go on to higher education. White working class pupils (particularly boys) are amongst the lowest performers. The link between poverty and attainment is multi-racial with socio-economic gaps much greater than those between different ethnic groups.

Effective assessment, tracking and feedback is essential throughout Key Stage 3 in order to ensure that every pupil achieves his or her potential and that attainment gaps are not allowed to widen. And yet, in most its inspections between 2013 and 2015, Ofsted found many schools neglect these three years of a child's education and are then forced to take remedial action at Key Stage 4.

As we already know, Ofsted's 2015 report KS3: The Wasted Years? claims that Key Stage 3 is not a high priority for secondary school leaders in terms of timetabling, assessment and the monitoring of pupils' progress. It also says that school leaders prioritise the pastoral over the academic needs of pupils during pupils' transition from primary school and that many secondary schools do not build sufficiently on pupils' prior learning. Finally, the report argues that schools are not using Pupil Premium funding effectively to close gaps quickly in Key Stage 3.

So how can schools improve the quality and effectiveness of assessment at Key Stage 3? How can they ensure that every pupil's progress is monitored and that interventions are put into place in a timely manner as soon as a pupil's progress falters? And how can schools be sure that those interventions are the most effective strategies to use and offer the best value for money for the public purse?

Using data

In an earlier chapter in this book on cross-phase partnerships I explained that data is more than just a spreadsheet, it is a conversation. Whereas most secondary teachers will already have access to some information about their new Year 7s including which primary school they came from, the scaled scores they achieved on their Key Stage 2 tests and, if they delve into the question level analysis, the marks they received for individual questions in those tests, a pupil's Year 6 teacher will know so much more than these numbers can possibly say. They'll know, for example, what the pupil can achieve when they're not under test conditions and what particular topics they've studied and found interesting. They'll know what their attitude to learning is like and what skills they've developed over their first seven years of schooling. They'll know what extra-curricular activities they've taken part in and how well they did, as well as what motivates them to succeed and what demotivates them. They'll know, too, what their home life is like and what obstacles they've had to overcome and might still be facing daily. So, yes, data is more than a spreadsheet. Recognising assessment in its widest sense - and taking information from as many sources as possible - enables data to become a rich and meaningful conversation.

The effective use of data - to monitor and evaluate pupil progress and facilitate these rich conversations - lies at the heart of good assessment. But what does it look like in practice?

Good data management means identifying and unpicking the data in order to analyse the progress of pupil groups. Good data management means auditing the effectiveness of past and current interventions. Good data management means discussing barriers with staff and pupils, asking them what do they think are the priorities. It means raising the profile of research and potential solutions, using external evidence of what works, identifying the tools and strategies that are needed.

Good data management means building leadership capacity to make sustainable improvements and strengthen the school's own performance capability. It means developing a plan and demonstrating the links to the school's core aims.

Data in Key Stage 3 needs to be used to close the gaps between the performances of different groups of pupils, particularly - as we heard at the start of this chapter - those from disadvantaged socio-economic backgrounds. So how can we do this?

Diminishing the difference

Firstly, when it comes to closing the gap (or, in Ofsted's new parlance, 'diminishing the difference') between the educational achievement of different groups of pupils, what matters most is pedagogy - if we get the teaching and learning in the classroom right first time, then there is less need of interventions later.

In particular, what works best at Key Stage 3 for closing the gap is structured phonics instruction, cooperative learning approaches, frequent assessment and feedback, and the explicit teaching of metacognition. Contrary to popular opinion, the traditional use of ICT in the classroom has only modest gains although the use of whole-class ICT (such as the interactive whiteboard, embedded multimedia, etc.) is more effective than the use of individualised, self-instructional ICT programmes. Classroom management strategies - such as the use of a rapid pace of instruction, all-pupil responses, and a common language of discipline - help to close the gap, too, as does the use of one to one tutoring for struggling readers.

Other proven whole-school approaches to closing the gap include:
- Rigorous monitoring and the use of data
- Raising pupil aspirations using engagement programmes
- Engaging parents and raising parental aspirations
- Developing social and emotional competencies
- Coaching teachers and teaching assistants in specific strategies such as cooperative learning, frequent assessment and metacognition

In order to close the gap, school leaders need to ensure that there is enhanced collaboration and communication between staff both within and between partner schools. This may necessitate the development of leadership skills among some staff and helping teachers to improve their understanding of alternative contexts and ways of dealing with similar issues. Teachers may also need help developing a better awareness of the barriers to learning that some pupils face and an understanding of the attainment gaps. Another important strategy for closing the gap is to increase parental involvement, both in terms of enlisting their support with homework and in helping to raise pupil aspirations and expectations.

Life after levels

Assessment in Key Stage 3 should emulate that in Key Stage 4 - in other words, there should be the same rigour and determination to assess, monitor and track pupil progress in Years 7, 8 and 9 as there is in Years 10 and 11, and the tracking data should be used just as frequently and robustly to identify pupils whose progress has faltered and to put in place intervention strategies to support them.

However, there is one key difference. At Key Stage 4 assessment takes the form of GCSE grades. At Key Stage 3, life has been made a little more complicated by the scrapping of national curriculum levels as a statutory requirement. So, let us look at what the government says about assessment in Key Stage 3 now that we live in a life after levels...

The Department for Education has made clear that each school is autonomous and can develop its own system of assessment. Whatever system it develops should be fair and transparent, and it should set high expectations for the attainment and progress of all pupils. The Department for Education says that assessment should be the servant and not the master of excellent teaching and, what matters most, is that schools provide high value qualifications and teach a broad and balanced curriculum.

In Years 7 and 8, schools are expected to engage in ongoing formative assessment of pupils although this is not a statutory requirement. They are also expected to provide periodic progress checks (again, this is non-statutory). Schools are also expected to summatively assess pupils against end of year outcomes although, once again, this is non-statutory. In fact, the only statutory duty in Years 7 and 8 is to report once a year to parents in some form.

In Year 9, schools are also expected to engage in ongoing formative assessment which is again a not a statutory duty. They are also expected to provide periodic progress checks (again, this is non-statutory). The key difference is that, in Year 9, the expectation that schools summatively assess pupils against end of key stage outcomes is a statutory requirement, as is the requirement to report to parents.

Although the statutory duties placed on schools are somewhat limited, it is good practice to ensure that pupil progress is regularly observed and analysed and that the data is shared with all interested parties - parents, staff and governors. It is also good practice to ensure that the data that is gathered from this process is used - not just to report progress - but in a number of other important ways. For example, progress data should be used to identify underperforming groups and then to direct the appropriate deployment of staff and resources to support those groups to close the gap. Progress data should also be used to inform teachers' target-setting activity, ensuring targets are aspirational but achievable. Finally, progress data should be used to monitor the impact of strategies and interventions and those interventions which are found not to be working well enough should be stopped or improved and then re-evaluated.

In the best schools, there are well-developed pupil tracking systems at work in Key Stage 3 as well as in Key Stage 4 which capture a wider range of data than just attainment levels. These schools also use external data and self-evaluation in order to focus on the gaps and on pupil progress, not just on average attainment. As well as informing staff on pupil progress, these schools use data to provide pupils with regular feedback on their progress.

In Chapter Sixteen we'll take a closer look at how your school might respond to 'life after levels'...

CHAPTER SIXTEEN
Assessment without levels

The Commission for Assessment Without Levels, in their 2015 report, claimed that the use of levels led to a curriculum driven by targets which, in turn, came to dominate all forms of in-school assessment and had a profoundly negative impact on teaching and learning.

As a result, progress - they said - became synonymous with moving up to the next 'level' or 'sub-level'. But this posed a problem: progress - in real terms - involves developing a deeper and broader understanding of subject matter, not simply moving on to work that affords a greater level of difficulty.

The Commission also said that, as a consequence of National Curriculum levels becoming synonymous with assessment, the more informal, everyday formative assessment that should always have been an integral part of effective teaching at Key Stage 3 was largely abandoned. Instead, teachers were simply tracking pupils' progress towards target levels rather than engaging in genuine dialogue with pupils about what they had mastered and what they still needed to practice.

One of the other problems with this approach was that the language of levels did not lend itself to assessing the underpinning knowledge and understanding of a concept. Level descriptors offered pseudo-scientific and ostensibly precise measurements which, when analysed, offer little help to pupils in their quest to know how to improve.

Removing the 'label' of levels, the Commission suggested, could help to improve pupils' mindsets about their own ability...

Once levels have been removed, teachers - in reviewing their teaching and assessment strategies - could then aim to ensure that they used methods that allowed all pupils full access to the curriculum.

The Commission also claimed that the expectation placed on teachers to collect data in order to track pupils' progress towards target levels and sub-levels considerably increases teachers' workloads. Without levels, the Commission said, teachers would gradually increase their confidence in using a wider range of formative assessment strategies without the burden of unnecessary recording and tracking.

Removing levels would also shine a brighter spotlight on high quality formative assessment, thereby improving the quality of teaching, as well as contributing to raising standards and reinforcing schools' freedoms to deliver a quality education in the way that best suits the needs of their pupils and the strengths and skills of their staff.

The Commission therefore recommended that schools developed an alternative to levels that marked a definitive departure from the prevailing culture rather than replicated the existing system in all but name. They strongly hinted that schools should base their new assessment systems on the mastery learning approach developed by Benjamin Bloom in the 1960s. This makes sense because the new National Curriculum also has mastery learning at its core.

In Bloom's version of 'mastery', learning is broken down into discrete units and is presented in a logical order. Pupils are required to demonstrate a comprehensive knowledge of each unit before being allowed to move on to the next unit, the assumption being that all pupils will achieve this level of mastery if they are appropriately supported: some may take longer and need more help, but all will get there in the end.

Designing a new system

In a moment we will explore how a school could build a new assessment system to replace levels based on the concept of mastery learning but first we must take a step back...

Before a school can agree a new assessment system - whether it designs one in-house or purchases one 'off the peg' so to speak - it should make sure it has written, consulted upon and agreed a whole-school assessment policy. This policy should then be ratified by the governing body or academy sponsors. From this point forwards, the assessment policy should be the school's guiding light; everything the school does to develop an alternative to levels should support the delivery of this policy.

Once a new assessment policy is in place, a school needs to decide what unit of measurement will replace National Curriculum levels. In other words, how will the school describe pupils' learning and progress? Whatever measure a school decides to use, it must successfully quantify learning and progress and must do so in a more meaningful way than levels and sub-levels did, or else why change?

So where should a school start?

Some schools I've worked with or spoken to during the course of writing this book have made the mistake of developing a new assessment system - and grade descriptors to quantify pupil performance - on the false assumption that their existing schemes of work will adequately cover the Subject Content in the new National Curriculum. In other words, they have begun by designing a new unit of measurement to replace levels before considering how they will plan and teach the new National Curriculum. The result has been a system of 'levels' in all but name.

Schools should start by engaging in a process of detailed curriculum planning before they set about designing a system of assessment. After all, how can you decide on your assessment criteria before you know what it is you're assessing? How we teach the National Curriculum and how pupils respond to it should form the basis of any new assessment system and that system should be based on new schemes of work. Those schemes of work should, in turn, be written in line with the new National Curriculum.

What's more, assessment systems which simply recreate grading similar to levels and sub-levels are, to my mind, missing the point.

The new National Curriculum is a description of the content that must be taught in each subject and should, therefore, be a school's starting point in deciding upon the units of measurement it will use to quantify learning and progress.

A school's first task, therefore, should be to convert the content described in the National Curriculum into schemes of work which describe what will be taught and what learning will result. This kind of detailed curriculum planning is necessary if a school is to successfully develop assessment criteria. Schools should not make the mistake of rushing into designing a new assessment system before they've considered how the National Curriculum will be taught in practice.

A school's second task, then, is to understand how a pupil's knowledge and skills in those parts of the subject covered in a particular scheme of work will accumulate over the course of Key Stage 3 into a holistic understanding of the concepts, key ideas, and capabilities learnt in the subject. As such, schemes of work need to be progressive in nature, developing gradually over time.

Only once the National Curriculum has been converted into schemes of work and everyone is clear about how pupils' knowledge and skills will develop over the course of those schemes of work, can a school move on to the third and final task: to develop a means of describing and quantifying what pupils are learning as they move through the schemes of work.

So, to summarise:

1. Convert the National Curriculum into schemes of work covering the year and key stage
2. Understand how knowledge and skills will accumulate over the year and key stage
3. Develop a system for describing and quantifying pupils' learning in each scheme of work, year and key stage

Let's now turn our attentions to how this will work in practice and to how we might quantify pupils' learning...

Putting it into practice

The Commission for Assessment Without Levels were clear in their report that 'life after levels' should be less bureaucratic for teachers. Teachers should spend more time engaged in formative classroom assessments with pupils and less time tracking and recording data. As such, a majority of the assessments that take place in Key Stage 3 should be informal, leading to diagnostic feedback given to pupils either in writing in their exercise books or verbally in lessons. Naturally, this data will either be unrecorded or held locally in teachers' mark-books.

Diagnostic feedback should be comment-only and be specific about what pupils need to do in order to improve. In an earlier chapter about the Conditions for Learning, I explained that the best feedback addresses faulty interpretations and comments on rather than grades work. I also said that the best feedback provides cues or prompts for further work, is timely, specific and clear, and is focused on task and process rather than on praising. Feedback also works best when it is explicit about the marking criteria, offers suggestions for improvement, and is focused on how pupils can close the gap between their current and their desired performance; it does not focus on presentation or quantity of work.

Occasionally, however, it will be necessary for teachers to reflect on how well their pupils are responding to what is being taught and to share this information more formally with their subject leaders, senior leaders, and other colleagues who teach the same class. This more formal assessment will need to take the form of progress against or towards targets - or perhaps age-related expectations - so what should it look like in practice?

The use of levels and sub-levels assumed that pupils scaled the mountain of progress in a uniform manner in response to teaching, and that we could measure each step with accuracy then categorise and label each pupil accordingly.

Mastery learning replaces this rush to hike up the mountainside with the belief that all pupils will comprehensively know and understand the learning from each unit before moving on to the next. Progress, therefore, tends to be non-linear and tailored to meet the needs of each pupil.

'Progress' is a complex concept - a dotted line used to summarise the overall path taken along the mountainside, snaking towards the peak, which may go up as well as down as pupils find the right terrain and get a solid foothold in the rock. But, statistically-speaking, we can estimate the average grade that a pupil can achieve based on their prior performance and this information can be used to notify us if pupils fall below expectations.

Intended learning outcomes provide a good starting start - a foundation, if you like - for tracking pupil progress because they summarise what is taught in each lesson or unit and they are already widely used in lesson planning and delivery. Teachers routinely write and share objectives with pupils at the start of lessons and use them to measure progress in lesson plenaries.

As long as intended learning outcomes cover all the statements in the National Curriculum Subject Content, then tracking and recording pupils' acquisition of them should provide a cumulative assessment log which will quantify their progress at any given point during Key Stage 3.

Once we reach the end of a scheme of work, or a sensible waypoint in a unit, a good way to express the extent to which pupils have mastered a set of intended learning outcomes is to categorise them as either 'Emerging', 'Developing', 'Secure' or 'Mastered'. Using only four categories like this - as opposed to myriad levels and sub-levels - provides a broad-brush approach which contrasts with the artificial precision provided by level descriptors.

These four categories can then by linked to GCSE grades to show the degree to which a pupil is 'GCSE ready'. For example, the word 'Emerging' could equate to GCSE grades 1 and 2, whilst 'Developing' could be pegged to GCSE grades 3 and 4. 'Secure', meanwhile, could be equivalent to GCSE grades 5 and 6, whereas 'Mastered' could equate to GCSE grades 7, 8 and 9.

CHAPTER SEVENTEEN
The Pupil Premium

The Pupil Premium is money given to schools to help disadvantaged pupils. Ofsted said that schools prioritise their Pupil Premium spending in Key Stage 4 and do not use the funding effectively in Key Stage 3 to ensure that gaps between disadvantaged pupils and their peers continue to close following the transition to secondary school. However, this is a vicious cycle because if you focus your time and resources in Key Stage 4, and thus neglect Key Stage 3, then the gap will widen in the intervening years and that time and money will be needed simply to compensate for ineffective practice in the earlier phase of secondary education. If, however, the Pupil Premium is used effectively at Key Stage 3 and pupils are supported through high quality teaching and interventions, then they will be provided with a better springboard to GCSE and fewer remedial actions will be needed in Years 10 and 11.

Before we look at how the Pupil Premium might best be utilised in Key Stage 3, let's be clear on who the funding is for and how it can legally be spent...

Pupil Premium funding is awarded to pupils who are categorised as 'Ever 6 FSM'. For the 2015/16 academic year, for example, the funding will be given to pupils who are recorded in the January 2015 school census who are known to have been eligible for free school meals (FSM) in any of the previous six years (in other words, since the summer of 2009), as well as those first known to be eligible in January 2015.

Pupil Premium funding is also awarded to pupils who are adopted from care or who have left care. For the 2015/16 academic year, for example, the funding will be given to pupils who are recorded in the January 2015 school census and alternative provision census who were looked after by an English or Welsh local authority immediately before being adopted, or who left local authority care on a special guardianship order or child arrangements order (previously known as a residence order).

Finally, Pupil Premium funding is awarded to pupils who are categorised as 'Ever 5 service child' which - for the purposes of the Pupil Premium grant conditions - means a pupil recorded in the January 2015 school census who was eligible for the service child premium in any of the previous four years (in other words, since the January 2011 school census) as well as those recorded as a service child for the first time on the January 2015 school census.

Pupil Premium is for the purposes of the school it is awarded to. In other words, it is for the educational benefit of pupils registered at that school. But it can also be used for the benefit of pupils registered at other maintained schools or academies and on community facilities such as services whose provision furthers any charitable purpose for the benefit of pupils at the school or their families, or people who live or work in the locality in which the school is situated. The money does not have to be completely spent by schools in the financial year it is awarded; some or all of it may be carried forward to future financial years.

The Pupil Premium and Ofsted

Schools are held to account for how they spend the money and the impact that money has on closing the gap. For example, Ofsted inspections report on how a school's use of the funding affects the attainment of their disadvantaged pupils and the DfE holds a school to account through performance tables, which include data on the attainment of pupils who attract the funding, the progress made by these pupils, and the gap in attainment between disadvantaged pupils and their peers.

Ofsted's Common Inspection Handbook (2015) explains that when judging the effectiveness of leadership and management, inspectors will consider: "How effectively leaders use additional funding, including the pupil premium, and measure its impact on outcomes for pupils, and how effectively governors hold them to account for this."

The Pupil Premium is also mentioned in the grade descriptors for leadership and management. The 'outstanding' grade descriptors, for example, include the following: "Governors systematically challenge senior leaders so that the effective deployment of staff and resources, including the pupil premium and special educational needs (SEN) funding, secures excellent outcomes for pupils. Governors do not shy away from challenging leaders about variations in outcomes for pupil groups, especially between disadvantaged and other pupils." In the 'good' grade descriptors, meanwhile, it says: "Governors hold senior leaders stringently to account for all aspects of the school's performance, including the use of pupil premium and SEN funding, ensuring that the skilful deployment of staff and resources delivers good or improving outcomes for pupils."

When preparing for an inspection, the lead inspector will analyse information on the school's website, including its statement on the use of the Pupil Premium. The lead inspector will also request that any reports following an external review of the school's use of the Pupil Premium are made available at the start of the inspection. During the inspection, inspectors will gather evidence about the use of the Pupil Premium in relation to the following: The level of Pupil Premium funding received by the school that academic year and in previous years; how the school has spent the money and why it has decided to spend it in the way it has; and any differences made to the learning and progress of disadvantaged pupils as shown by outcomes data and inspection evidence.

Inspectors will take particular account of the progress made by disadvantaged pupils by the end of the key stage compared with that made nationally by other pupils with similar starting points and the extent to which any gaps in this progress, and consequently in attainment, are closing. Inspectors will compare the progress and attainment of the school's disadvantaged pupils with the national figures for the progress and attainment of non-disadvantaged pupils. They will then consider in-school gaps between disadvantaged and non-disadvantaged pupils, and how much these gaps are closing. Inspectors will consider in-school gaps between disadvantaged and non-disadvantaged pupils.

It's worth noting that inspectors are likely to compare the progress of disadvantaged pupils with all non-disadvantaged pupils, not just with those who have similar starting points because if inspectors only compared the progress and attainment of pupils who started at a similar level, they would be unable to establish if gaps in attainment between disadvantaged and non-disadvantaged pupils were closing.

Inspectors will check that the reason the gap is narrowing is because the attainment and progress of disadvantaged pupils is rising, rather than that of non-disadvantaged pupils falling. If an attainment gap exists or widens, inspectors will also consider whether this is because disadvantaged pupils attain more highly than others do nationally, but non-disadvantaged pupils in the school attain even more highly. The Common Inspection Framework says "these circumstances would not reflect negatively on the school".

Key questions for Key Stage 3 leaders

In light of all this, I would recommend that leaders of Key Stage 3 prepare for any inspection or DfE visit by asking themselves the following questions:

1. Did I focus sufficiently on literacy and numeracy interventions?
2. Did I work with primary feeders to identify pupils who might benefit from summer schools, nurture groups, etc.?
3. Did I target my best teachers at my most disadvantaged pupils?
4. Did I apply for top-up summer school funding when it was available? (It was removed in 2016.)
5. Do all my teachers know who was eligible for Pupil Premium funding? Do they and governors know how that funding was used and what impact it has had?
6. Where do pupils do their homework and independent study? If they live in chaotic homes, do we provide a quiet space with support? Have I involved parents in making sure pupils use it?
7. What happened after I looked at the data? What interventions did it lead to and what was their impact? What have I learnt?
8. Did I have gaps between exclusion and attendance rates as well as attainment gaps?
9. Was a senior leader at my school responsible for Pupil Premium funding? Do we also have a governor responsible for it?
10. Did higher (and lower) attaining pupils make as much progress as non-FSM? (Remember, the Pupil Premium is not just there to get pupils up to age related minimum expectations.)
11. What did I use as a benchmark when I compared our performance to other schools? (Don't just compare FSM pupils to other FSM pupils; and look beyond LA figures to national standards.)
12. How did I evaluate pastoral interventions? Did I ensure that, ultimately, they led to academic improvements as well as improvements in, say, attendance and behaviour?
13. When did I review my interventions? Did I track, review and improve our provision as I went along rather than wait until the end?

The answers to these questions can provide the basis for your Pupil Premium action plan. So, ask yourself: What do you need to do now in order to be fully prepared for inspection?

Above all, as you prepare for inspection, remember this mantra: know thy impact!

Good practice

As you start working towards your action plan, what should you be aiming for? What's your end goal? What does good practice in this area look like?

Schools that use the Pupil Premium funding effectively at Key Stage 3 and close the gap tend to conduct a detailed analysis of where pupils are underachieving and why. They make good use of research evidence when choosing support and intervention activities but are discerning customers of research - they always contextualise the information, asking: How would this work in my school? And: What do I know already works in my context? Research is extremely valuable as a starting point but you must not underestimate your own knowledge of your school and its pupils and staff.

As well as applying research and personal knowledge, schools that use the Pupil Premium funding effectively at Key Stage 3 focus on high quality teaching rather than relying on interventions to compensate because they know that pedagogy trumps all - getting it right first time is the best approach and teaching matters more than curriculum. They ensure that their best teachers lead English and maths intervention groups. They make frequent use of achievement data in order to check the effectiveness of interventions and they do this early and continue to do it throughout the year rather than waiting until the intervention has finished and it's too late to change it.

These schools also tend to have a systematic focus on clear pupil feedback and pupils receive regular advice to help them improve their work. These schools have a designated senior leader with a clear overview of the funding allocation and a solid understanding of how the funding works and how it needs reporting. All the teachers in these schools are aware of the pupils who are eligible for Pupil Premium funding and they take responsibility for those pupils' progress. These schools have strategies in place for improving attendance, behaviour and links with families and communities if these are an issue, as well as for improving academic performance. And, finally, these schools ensure that the performance management of staff includes discussions about the Pupil Premium and about individual pupils in receipt of the funding and how they are progressing.

Common pitfalls

Conversely, in schools where the Pupil Premium isn't used effectively and is not tracked well enough, there tends to be a lack of clarity about the intended impact of interventions. These schools run the same intervention strategies year after year because that's just what they're used to doing or have the staff and resources for, irrespective of whether they work. There is no real monitoring of the quality and impact of the interventions and no real awareness of what works and what offers the best value for money. These schools also tend to spend the money indiscriminately on teaching assistants but TAs are not well utilised.

The schools whose Pupil Premium practice is ineffective also tend to have an unclear audit trail and focus solely on pupils attaining the Level 4 benchmarks not higher. They tend to spend the Pupil Premium in isolation, it does not feature as part of the whole school development plan and decisions about it are not therefore taken in the round. These schools also compare their performance to local, not national, data. Pupil Premium funding is used for pastoral interventions but they are vague and not focused on desired outcomes for pupils. And, finally, in these schools, governors are not involved in taking decisions about Pupil Premium spending and are not informed about its use and impact.

What to report

Schools need to report on how much Pupil Premium funding they received in the current academic year and how they intend to spend the funding. They need to be able to articulate their reasons and evidence for this. Schools also need to report on how they spent the funding they received for the last academic year and what difference it made to the attainment of disadvantaged pupils.

The funding is allocated for each financial year, but the information schools publish online should refer to the academic year as this is how parents and the public understand the school year. As schools won't know how much funding they're getting for the latter part of the academic year (from April to July), they should report on the funding up to the end of the financial year then update the information when they have all the data.

If the school receives Year 7 literacy and numeracy catch-up premium funding, they must also publish details of how they spend this funding and the effect this has had on the attainment of the pupils who attract it.

CHAPTER EIGHTEEN
Numeracy

As we discovered in Chapter One, Ofsted do not believe that Key Stage 3 is a high enough priority for many secondary school leaders in terms of timetabling, assessment and the monitoring of pupils' progress.

In particular, inspectors have expressed concerns about the development of pupils' numeracy skills. A majority of the headteachers Ofsted spoke to when compiling The Wasted Years report were able to explain how they were improving literacy at Key Stage 3 but only a quarter could do the same for numeracy. This was reflected in inspection evidence, for example from monitoring inspections, where inspectors reported improvements in literacy nearly three times more than they did in numeracy.

Ofsted recommended that school leaders put in place numeracy strategies that ensure pupils build on their prior attainment in Key Stage 2.

It's true that many schools already have a clear focus on literacy and that it is numeracy that needs to be given greater priority and focus. But there is always room for improvement where literacy is concerned and there can be no issue more critical for schools to tackle.

Indeed, as Ofsted said in their 2012 report 'Moving English Forward', "There can be no more important subject than English in the school curriculum." The report went on to say:

"English is a pre-eminent world language, it is at the heart of our culture and it is the language medium in which most of our pupils think and communicate. Literacy skills are also crucial to pupils' learning in other subjects across the curriculum."

Literacy is critical to schools because, as a European Union report explained in 2012, "If smart growth is about knowledge and innovation, investment in literacy skills is a prerequisite for achieving such growth." The report added:

"Our world is dominated by the written word, both online and in print. This means we can only contribute and participate actively if we can read and write sufficiently well. But, each year, hundreds of thousands of children start their secondary school two years behind in reading; some leave even further behind their peers... Literacy is about people's ability to function in society as private individuals, active citizens, employees or parents... Literacy is about people's self-esteem, their interaction with others, their health and employability. Ultimately, literacy is about whether a society is fit for the future."

Moreover, in 2010 the National Literacy Trust published a report called 'Literacy: State of the Nation, A Picture of Literacy in the UK Today' in which it reported that 92% of the British public considered literacy to be vital to the economy and essential to getting a good job.

The Ofsted report 'Removing Barriers to Literacy' (2011) concludes that "teachers in a secondary school need to understand that literacy is a key issue regardless of the subject taught". The report goes on to say that literacy is an important element of teachers' effectiveness and that literacy supports learning because "pupils need vocabulary, expression and organisational control to cope with the cognitive demands of all subjects". It also argues that writing helps pupils to "sustain and order thought", that "better literacy leads to improved self-esteem, motivation and behaviour", and that literacy "allows pupils to learn independently" and is therefore "empowering". Moreover, it argues that "better literacy raises pupils' attainment in all subjects".

In 'Outstanding Literacy: A Teacher's Guide to Literacy Across the Curriculum' (2014), Matilda Rose argues: "Every teacher is a teacher of literacy. As a teacher of, say, Science, you have a responsibility to help your pupils learn about science, but you also have a responsibility to help them speak, read and write like a scientist ... It means having an analytical self-awareness, which enables you to identify how you speak, read and write about science ... And this is best done by explaining, demonstrating, modelling, teaching, and giving feedback."

So, although literacy may assume a higher priority than numeracy at Key Stage 3, there is still room for improvement. As such, in the next chapter, we will explore what effective literacy across the curriculum looks like in practice. But first let us turn to the more pressing issue of numeracy...

Numeracy across the curriculum

Numeracy is often regarded as literacy's poor relation, not given the same amount of time, resources and priority as its close cousin.

After years of investment and a war of attrition, most teachers now understand their role in developing pupils' literacy skills because they recognise that English - reading, and writing, and speaking and listening, are the medium through which pupils learn and articulate their learning right across the curriculum. If they are not literate, pupils will not achieve in any subject.

However, many teachers still struggle to understand their role in developing pupils' numeracy skills and fail to see how their subject presents the same opportunities for embedding numeracy as it does for embedding literacy.

Let us first, then, look at what numeracy means in Key Stage 3 and provide some examples of numeracy at play in various subjects.

Numeracy can be meaningfully divided into four categories:
1. Handling information;
2. Space, shape and measurements;
3. Operations and calculations; and
4. Numbers.

Handling information is about graphs and charts, comparing sets of data and types of data, processing data, and probability. Within graphs and charts, you might look at pie and bar charts. You might look at interpreting information, you might look at data in lists and tables, and you might look at reading scales. Within comparing sets of data and types of data, you might look at measures of averages, measures of spread, discrete data and continuous data. Within processing data, you might look at decision trees and VENN diagrams. Within probability, you might look at using a probability scale, estimating probability from statistical information, and experimental probability.

Space, shape and measurements is about both space, shape and measure, and solving problems with space, shape and measure. Within measurements, you might look at standard units of measurements for length, mass, capacity, time, temperature, and area and perimeter, and consider both metric and imperial measurements. You might select and use measuring instruments and look at how to interpret numbers and read scales. You might also look at volume. Within shape and space, you might look at coordinates to describe a position. You might look at simple positional language. You might look at symmetry. You might look at 2D and 3D shapes. And you might look at angles. Solving problems with space, shape and measurements might involve selecting and using appropriate skills to solve geographical problems.

It might involve using geographical notation and symbols correctly.

Operations and calculations is about addition and subtraction, multiplication and division, number operations, and the effective use of calculators. Within addition and subtraction, you might look at knowing plus and minus facts to twenty, at mental methods to one hundred, and at whole numbers to one thousand and beyond. Within multiplication and division, you might look at knowing multiply and divide facts to twenty, and remainders and rounding. Within number operations you might look at inverse operations, interrelationships and order of operations. And within the effective use of calculators you might look some calculations with fractions, decimals and percentages, and calculations with negatives.

Numbers (and the use of the number system) is about using numbers, whole numbers, size and order, place value, patterns and sequences, and numbers 'in between' whole numbers. Within using numbers, you might look at reading and writing using symbols and labels, at ratio and proportion, at using numbers for measuring and for counting, and for ratio and proportion. Within whole numbers and size and order you might look at comparing and ordering and using number lines. Within place value you might look at zero as a place holder, at money context, at measures and at estimation. Within sequences and patterns, you might look at odd and even, at square numbers, at factors and multiples and at prime numbers. And within numbers 'in between' whole numbers you might look at fractions, decimals and percentages.

Numeracy encompasses three sets of skills:
1. Reasoning;
2. Problem-solving; and
3. Decision-making.

Reasoning might involve identifying structures, being systematic, searching for patterns, developing logical thinking, and predicting and checking. Problem-solving might involve identifying the information needed to carry out a task, breaking down a problem or task into smaller parts, interpreting solutions in context, and making mental estimates to check the reasonableness of an answer. And decision-making might involve choosing appropriate strategies, identifying relevant information and choosing the right tools and equipment.

In English, numeracy can be developed by using non-fiction texts which include mathematical vocabulary, graphs, charts and tables. In science, pupils will order numbers including decimals, calculate means, and percentages, use negative numbers when taking temperatures, substitute into formulae, rearrange equations, decide which graph to use to represent data, and plot, interpret and predict from graphs. In ICT, pupils will collect and classify data, enter it into data handling software to produce graphs and tables, and interpret and explain the results. When they use computer models and simulations they will draw on their abilities to manipulate numbers and identify patterns and relationships. In art and design and technology, pupils will use measurements and patterns, spatial ideas, the properties of shapes, and symmetry, and use multiplication and ratio to enlarge and reduce the size of objects. In history, geography and RE, pupils will collect data and use measurements of different kinds. They will study maps and use coordinates and ideas of angles, direction, position, scale, and ratio. And they will use timelines similar to number lines.

Hopefully, if you were in any doubt, you can already see how numeracy is a whole-school concern and encompasses skills that apply across the curriculum.

So how can we ensure that numeracy is taught effectively throughout the school at Key Stage 3?

At the whole-school level in Key Stage 3, you need to create a positive environment that celebrates numeracy and provides pupils with role models by celebrating the numeracy successes of older pupils. You also need to ensure that planned activities allow pupils to learn and practice their numeracy skills. You should publicly display examples of high quality numeracy work from across the curriculum around the school. And you should ensure that every department adheres to the school's numeracy policy.

Individual departments at Key Stage 3 should provide high quality exemplar materials and display examples of numeracy work within their subject context. Departments should also highlight opportunities for the use of numeracy within their subject and ensure that the learning materials that are presented to pupils match both their capability in the subject and their numerical demands.

Individual teachers of Key Stage 3 classes, meanwhile, should have high expectations of all their pupils and ensure that the numerical content of their lessons is of a high standard. They should encourage pupils to show their numerical working out where relevant and encourage the use of estimation, particularly for checking work. Teachers should also encourage pupils to write mathematically-correct statements and to vocalise their maths. They should also encourage pupils to use non-calculator methods wherever possible. Teachers and departments should inform the maths department as soon as possible if any numeracy problems are identified.

CHAPTER NINETEEN
Literacy

According to the National Literacy Trust's State of a Nation report, around 16% of England's adult population - that's 5.2 million adults - are "functionally illiterate". In other words, they wouldn't pass an English GCSE and have literacy levels at or below those expected of an 11-year-old.

The 2012 PISA report found that 17% of England's 15 year olds had not achieved the minimum level of proficiency in literacy and that the gap between our highest and lowest performers was significantly above average.

According to the OECD's International Survey of Adult Skills, the UK is the only OECD country where young adults do not have better literacy skills than those nearing retirement.

But why are levels of literacy so poor? One reason is that is vocabulary is critical to success in reading as well as academic achievement more generally. The size of a pupil's vocabulary in their early years of schooling (the number and variety of words that the young person knows) is a significant predictor of reading comprehension in later schooling and in life.

Most children are experienced speakers of the language when they begin school but reading the language requires more complex, abstract vocabulary than that used in everyday conversation.

Children who have had stories read to them during the first years of their lives are exposed to a much broader and richer vocabulary than those contained in everyday conversations and, as such, arrive at school better prepared for reading. For this reason, we all need to understand the importance of vocabulary and support its development so that children who are not exposed to books before they start school are helped to catch up. Our understanding of a word grows with repeated exposure to it.

Dale & O'Rourke say that learning vocabulary takes place on a continuum, ranging from never having seen or heard a word before to having a deep knowledge of that word and its different meanings, as well as the ability to use that word confidently and accurately in both speaking and writing.

Acquiring vocabulary is incremental because words differ in many ways:

- They differ according to syntax – knowing what part of speech a particular word is can assist reading;
- They differ according to the size of their 'family' – knowing one of a family of words will help the reader determine a number of others;
- Some words are polysemous which means they can have multiple meanings (e.g. the word 'scale' means to climb, a feature of a fish, a plant disease, a measuring instrument, the ratio of distance on a map to that on the ground, and so on.

Pupils who know multiple meanings of words are more prepared to read widely and across multiple contexts. In short, vocabulary is complex but also vital to developing reading comprehension. If a pupil knows the meaning of the word happy, and knows the single letter-sounds that make that word, then the word can be easily decoded and understood when read in a text. The words happier and happiness are also more likely to be read and understood. With only a few exposures, these words will be familiar enough to be recognised on sight and so a pupil's reading vocabulary grows.

Young people who develop reading skills early in their lives by reading frequently add to their vocabularies exponentially over time. This is sometimes called 'The Matthew Effect' after the line in the Bible (Matthew 13:12), "The rich shall get richer and the poor shall get poorer". In the context of literacy, the Matthew Effect is that 'the word rich get richer while the word poor get poorer'.

In his book, also called The Matthew Effect, Daniel Rigney explains: "While good readers gain new skills very rapidly, and quickly move from learning to read to reading to learn, poor readers become increasingly frustrated with the act of reading, and try to avoid reading where possible.

"Pupils who begin with high verbal aptitudes find themselves in verbally enriched social environments and have a double advantage. Good readers may choose friends who also read avidly while poor readers seek friends with whom they share other enjoyments."

Furthermore, E D Hirsch, in his book The Schools We Need, says that "The children who possess intellectual capital when they first arrive at school have the mental scaffolding and Velcro to catch hold of what is going on, and they can turn the new knowledge into still more Velcro to gain still more knowledge".

Department for Education research suggests that, by the age of seven, the gap in the vocabulary known by children in the top and bottom quartiles is something like 4,000 words (children in the top quartile know around 7,000 words). The word poor cannot catch up with the word rich because to do so they'd need to be able to learn more words more quickly than the word rich. A pupil who does not know the meaning of the word happy will struggle over that and related words (e.g. happiness, happier, happiest, unhappy) in connected text, even if she can decode them, because transforming letters into words is useless if those words do not have a meaning.

If a pupil continues to experience frustration when reading because she is word poor, then she is likely to give up, denying herself of the opportunity to build vocabulary, fluency and world knowledge.

Young people who do not acquire these skills easily will become increasingly disadvantaged over time. Vocabulary helps to build comprehension and is therefore a key tool for reading. Young people who lack vocabulary and prior knowledge (context) will have difficulty understanding the books they encounter in school, especially as those books become more difficult.

So, what can we do to help the word poor become richer?

One answer is to plan group work activities which provide an opportunity for the word poor to mingle with the word rich, to hear language being used by pupils of their own age and in ways that they might not otherwise encounter.

Another answer is to model higher-order reading skills because, as the literate adults in the room, we teachers use these skills unconsciously all the time so we need to make the implicit explicit. For example, we could model:

- Moving quickly through and across texts
- Locating key pieces of information.
- Following the gist of articles
- Questioning a writer's facts or interpretation
- Linking one text with another
- Making judgments about whether one text is better than, more reliable than, or more interesting than another text

We can promote the love of reading for the sake of reading, too; encouraging our pupils to see reading as something other than a functional activity. It is the responsibility of every adult working in a school (not just teachers, and certainly not just English teachers) to show that reading because we like reading is one of the hallmarks of civilised adult life.

And another answer is to teach reading behaviours...

Research tells us there are four behaviours associated with good reading comprehension:

Firstly, good readers understand the purpose of reading, and so can adjust their reading style accordingly. In other words, they know why they are reading and how they should read. They can skim the contents page, chapter headings, and paragraph openings to get the gist of a text and to extract key information which enables them to interpret what a text means based on their prior knowledge.

Secondly, good readers understand the purpose of the text: Good readers are not only purposeful themselves, but they also understand that writers are purposeful. A writer may wish to provide very simple information (e.g. instructions for assembling a cabinet) or more complex information (e.g. a report on stem cell research). A writer may wish to persuade, inform or entertain the reader. A writer may wish to present opinions as indisputable fact. Understanding a writer's purpose makes good readers aware of how particular literary devices are being used to influence their response.

Thirdly, good readers review their comprehension: Good readers constantly review, analyse and assess their comprehension in order to ensure there are no gaps in their understanding. They relate information in a text to their own experiences or prior knowledge, and evaluate information in order to determine whether it confirms or contradicts what they already know. This is known as schema theory. Good readers ask questions as they read and search for the answers in the text.

And finally, good readers adjust their reading strategies: Good readers can adjust their reading strategies, slowing their reading speed when sentences are long and complex, re-reading a section if they begin to lose meaning, and drawing inferences from surrounding text or using their letter-sound knowledge in order to help construct the meaning of unfamiliar words. Good readers can also pause to take notes which help them retain complex information.

To help the word poor develop these four behaviours, we can do the following...

Before reading, we can:

- Explore what pupils already know about the topic of the text.
- Relate pupils' own experiences to the text.
- Ask pupils to make predictions about the text based on the title and any illustrations, this helps build background knowledge and increases their motivation for reading.
- Ask pupils to tell you about any other texts they've read on the same topic.
- Explicitly teach any new vocabulary pupils are likely to encounter, especially words which are crucial to understanding the text.

Whilst reading, we can:

- Read most of the text - particularly important parts of it - without lots of interruptions so that pupils can understand the plot and structure (following a sequence of events) and so that pupils can attune to the written style. Asking questions before and after reading the text are more effective and less intrusive than questions asked during reading.
- Signpost the new vocabulary you taught before reading.

- Pause occasionally - where appropriate - to gauge pupils' reactions: ask for comments, questions and predictions.
- Teach pupils strategies for regaining the meaning of a text when they begin to struggle or lose interest: e.g. reread the sentence carefully, think about what might make sense; reread the sentence before and after the one you're stuck on, look for familiar words inside or around an unfamiliar word.
- Teach pupils to monitor their understanding of the text by using post-it notes or page-markers. Post-it notes could be to used in order to: indicate a connection between the text and a prior experience or piece of knowledge, as well as between the text and another text; identify information which surprised them; and highlight something pupils want to ask later.

After reading, we can:

- Teach pupils how to identify the key words in a passage (the words that explain who, what, where, when, how or why).
- Teach pupils note-making - as opposed to note-taking - skills and other ways of summarising information such as graphic organisers (e.g. story maps, timelines, flow charts, plot profiles, etc.).
- Ask questions that help pupils to identify a sequence of events.
- Teach pupils to look out for cause and effect relationships.
- Ask pupils to rewrite the text in a different form: for example, from a diary to a time-line, from a set of instructions to a flow chart, from a piece of descriptive writing to a drawing.
- Teach pupils to use reference material such as a dictionary and thesaurus, a glossary and bibliography.

In 1993 Graham & Wong developed the 3H strategy for developing pupils' comprehension. The 3 Hs in question are: Here, Hidden, and Head. Moving pupils through the three stages takes them from literal to deductive questions.

'Here' questions are literal questions, the answers to which are apparent in the text. For example, 'What was the Stable Buck called in Of Mice and Men?

'Hidden' questions require pupils to synthesise information from different parts of a text. For example, 'How did Curley's Wife's life change when she got married?'

'Head' questions require pupils to use their prior knowledge in order to predict or deduce. For example, 'Do you think George ever really believed he'd own his own ranch? Why do you think that?'

So, one way in which we can close the literacy gap between the rich and poor is by helping the word poor to become richer by passing on our love of reading, and by making the implicit explicit, the invisible visible.

What else can we do to develop pupils' literacy skills in Key Stage 3...?

Literacy needs to be interwoven into the fabric of everyday school life and involve all staff. It should feature in all the school's development plans and be visible around the school. Literacy should also be a part of all meeting agenda and be regularly discussed at all levels. It always helps if there is a senior leader with literacy and pedagogy knowledge who champions literacy across the curriculum.

A school also needs an effective assessment system which sets literacy targets from national rather than local data. Literacy needs to be taught within a meaningful and relevant curriculum and this might involve the use of a quality phonics programme. Pupils identified as being 'at risk' for literacy should also have a nominated learning mentor. Schools need to develop good partnerships with parents, particularly for pupils who have high needs.

In the classroom, teachers need to allow time for pupils to share and recommend books. It helps if the school recruits influential readers, perhaps older pupils, teachers or volunteers. Local sportspeople are always keen to get involved and act as positive role models. The school should develop and maintain a calendar of reading events to which all departments contribute. All departments should give pupils literacy-targeted rewards such as book vouchers. Teachers of all subjects need to explicitly teach reading skills such as scanning, skimming, and reading for details when relevant to the assignment being set rather than expecting pupils to employ these skills independently and as if through a process of osmosis.

Teachers of all subjects should use Directed Activities Related to Texts (DARTs) to help pupils make sense of a text. For example, cloze (where words are missing from a text and pupils have to fill in the gaps), text marking, sequencing, and text reconstruction are all useful strategies.

Teachers need to engage pupils by linking what they are reading to the world beyond the classroom. They can also vary the way texts are read and by whom the texts are read.

Teachers need to give pupils a real audience, context and purpose for any writing tasks they set and should, where possible, give pupils an opportunity to embed the use of technology - such as blogs and social media - into their writing.

Literacy leaders need to teach the knowledge of texts (such as genre, text types, etc.) to all their teaching staff in order to enable teachers to know what features to focus on when planning and teaching reading and writing in their subjects.

Teachers of all subjects need to give pupils sufficient time to complete an extended piece of writing. The process of writing should include crafting and editing and pupils need to be explicitly taught how to draft, edit, and redraft work.

The school needs to develop a consistent policy and approach to teaching spelling, punctuation and grammar (SPaG) and teachers of all subjects need to explicitly teach SPaG in context, linked to the form of writing being developed at the time. To make this work in practice, literacy leaders will need to help all their teaching staff develop their own knowledge.

Teachers should use talk and discussion in order to illustrate the application and effect of grammar and they should develop pupils' knowledge of spelling strategies as well as the rules of spelling. Teachers in all subjects should take a consistent approach to marking spelling.

Teachers in all subjects should use a range of formal talk in lessons and should construct or co-construct with pupils the rules for speaking and listening such as turn-taking, making eye contact, active listening, and so on. Teachers need to make sure all pupils contribute to class discussion by prompting and directing them. Finally, all teachers need to model good speaking and listening skills during class discussions.

Part Six

End Matter

CHAPTER TWENTY
Conclusion

In Chapter One I explained that Ofsted's report Key Stage 3: The Wasted Years? found that, while pupils generally had the opportunity to study a broad range of subjects throughout Key Stage 3, in too many schools the quality of teaching and the rate of pupils' progress and achievement were not good enough.

Inspectors reported concerns about the effectiveness of Key Stage 3 in one in five of the routine inspections, particularly in relation to the slow progress made in English and maths and the lack of challenge for the most able pupils. Inspectors also reported significant weaknesses in MFL, history and geography at Key Stage 3. Too often, inspectors found teaching that failed to challenge and engage pupils. Additionally, low-level disruption in some of these lessons, particularly in MFL, had a detrimental impact on the pupils' learning. Achievement was not good enough in just under half of the MFL classes observed, two-fifths of the history classes and one third of the geography classes.

The report claimed that the weaknesses inspectors identified in teaching and pupil progress reflect a general lack of priority given to Key Stage 3 by many secondary school leaders. Most leaders spoken to as part of the survey, the report said, admitted they staffed Key Stages 4 and 5 before Key Stage 3. Thus, some Key Stage 3 classes were split between more than one teacher or were taught by non-specialists. In this sense - and in the way schools monitored and assessed pupils' progress - Key Stage 3 was a poor relation to the other key stages.

The report also asserted that too many secondary schools did not work effectively with partner primary schools to understand pupils' prior learning and ensure that they built on this during Key Stage 3. Some secondary leaders simply accepted that pupils would repeat what they had already done in primary school during the early part of Key Stage 3, particularly in Year 7. In addition, half of the pupils surveyed said that their homework never, or only some of the time, helped them to make progress. And inspectors found that, too often, homework did not consolidate or extend pupils' learning.

The report claimed that some school leaders did not use the Pupil Premium effectively in Key Stage 3 to ensure that gaps between disadvantaged pupils and their peers continued to close following transition to secondary school. Instead, additional support tended to be focused on intervention activities at Key Stage 4, which by then would have to compensate for ineffective practice in the earlier years of secondary education.

The report's key findings were as follows:

- Key Stage 3 is not a high priority for many secondary school leaders in timetabling, assessment and monitoring of pupils' progress. Eighty-five per cent of senior leaders interviewed said that they staff Key Stages 4 and 5 before Key Stage 3. Key Stage 3 is given lower priority, where classes are more often split between more than one teacher or where pupils are taught by non-specialists.
  - o Leaders prioritise the pastoral over the academic needs of pupils during transition from primary school. While this affects all pupils, it can have a particularly detrimental effect on the progress and engagement of the most able.
  - o Many secondary schools do not build sufficiently on pupils' prior learning. Many of the senior leaders interviewed said that they do not do this well enough and accepted that some pupils would repeat some of what they had done in Key Stage 2.
  - o Some school leaders are not using the Pupil Premium funding effectively to close gaps

quickly in Key Stage 3. Inspection evidence and senior leaders' comments indicate that this is another area where Key Stage 4 often takes priority.

o Developing pupils' literacy skills in Key Stage 3 is a high priority in many schools but the same level of priority is not evident for numeracy. A majority of the headteachers Ofsted spoke to were able to explain how they were improving literacy at Key Stage 3 but only a quarter could do the same for numeracy. This is reflected in inspection evidence, for example in monitoring inspections inspectors reported improvements in literacy nearly three times more often than they did in numeracy.

o Homework is not consistently providing the opportunities for pupils to consolidate or extend their learning in Key Stage 3. Approximately half of the pupils who responded to Ofsted's online questionnaire said that their homework never, or only some of the time, helps them to make progress.

In concluding their report, Ofsted recommended senior leaders should make Key Stage 3 a higher priority in all aspects of school planning, monitoring and evaluation, and ensure that not only is the curriculum offer at Key Stage 3 broad and balanced, but that teaching is of high quality and prepares pupils for more challenging subsequent study at Key Stages 4 and 5.

Ofsted also recommended that senior leaders ensure that transition from Key Stage 2 to 3 focuses as much on pupils' academic needs as it does on their pastoral needs, and that senior leaders foster better cross-phase partnerships with primary schools in order to ensure that Key Stage 3 teachers build on pupils' prior knowledge, understanding and skills.

Ofsted said middle and senior leaders should make sure that systems and procedures for assessing and monitoring pupils' progress in Key Stage 3 are more robust and that leaders should focus on the needs of disadvantaged pupils in Key Stage 3, including the most able, in order to close the achievement gap as quickly as possible. Leaders should also evaluate the quality and effectiveness of homework in Key Stage 3 in order to ensure that it helps pupils to make good progress. And finally, school leaders should put in place literacy and numeracy strategies that ensure pupils build on their prior attainment in Key Stage 2 in these crucial areas.

In Chapter One I explained that whilst all of Ofsted's recommendations were sensible and worthwhile, they were also - perhaps understandably for a high-level report - vague and intangible. For example, what does it mean, in reality, to give Key Stage 3 a high priority? What, in practice, do cross-phase partnerships look like? What is robust assessment and monitoring, exactly? And what, precisely, constitutes quality and effective homework?

This book was my attempt at answering those questions and more besides. Throughout, I have argued that the secret to an effective Key Stage 3 is to:

Make transition count by ensuring that pupils are supported to transfer - not just between the different phases of education as they move from primary to secondary, but also between all the key stages and years of compulsory schooling as pupils transfer between Years 7, 8 and 9 - gradually and smoothly;

Make the curriculum count by ensuring that there is a greater sense of continuity between primary and secondary schools both in terms of what is taught and when it is taught, and by ensuring that the way in which the curriculum is taught is challenging, engaging and different to that which precedes and succeeds it, and provides for the effective development of literacy and numeracy skills;

Make homework count by ensuring that homework enables pupils to practice their prior learning, provides a real audience, purpose and context, and is an optimum volume to support and yet not demotivate pupils;

Make data count by improving the quality and effectiveness of target-setting, assessment, and tracking in order to ensure that the regular monitoring of progress leads to frequent, formative feedback, and timely interventions and support which seek to diminish any differences in the performance of different groups of pupils.

I hope that we are now able to confidently and robustly answer the question that forms the title of Ofsted's report - KS3: The Wasted Years? - with a firm and frank 'no'. By way of conclusion, though, let me end with six features of an effective Key Stage 3 transition and induction process, each littered with suggestions of further reading. I am indebted to the Department for Education for many of the reports cited in this chapter.

Feature 1 - Collaborate before and after pupils transfer from primary school

Research shows that collaboration between primary and secondary schools both before and after pupils transfer from Year 6 into Year 7 is an important feature of a smooth and effective transition process. The Department for Education (then called the Department for Children, Schools and Families) carried out research in 2008 across seven local authorities involving forty-seven primary and secondary schools (including some special schools) to explore what could strengthen their transfer and transition practices. The final report concluded that effective transfer did not involve one key stage 'doing' transfer to the next, but an equal partnership that had professionally developed all stakeholders.

Likewise, Galton et al. (1999, 2003) highlighted the importance of Year 6 and Year 7 teachers working together to plan and teach "bridging units" (projects which were started towards the end of Year 6 and completed at the start of Year 7) in order to help inform and personalise the pupil transfer experience.

Other examples of effective collaboration might include the establishment of cross-phase working processes both within and between children's services. It might include planning schemes of work that promote curriculum continuity and a consistency of teaching and learning styles. It might include the facilitation and support of local cross-phase networking meetings of families of schools to jointly plan for strengthening transfer and the joint working between teachers in different key stages to promote an understanding of pupils' abilities and levels of knowledge. Galton suggests work on planning and teaching bridging units should be jointly planned to maximise personalisation.

Feature 2 - Communicate effectively between the phases and with pupils/parents

Effective communication between teachers from different school/phases, and with parents/carers and pupils is key to improving the transition from primary to secondary school.

Effective communication between teachers from different school phases can be achieved by arranging regular visits by secondary teachers to primary school and, in return, visits by primary teachers to secondary school. These visits can take many forms including: Talks to pupils in assemblies and form time about their respective schools; taster lessons, especially opportunities for pupils to experience secondary school facilities such as science labs and design and technology workshops; teachers working together to plan lessons and discuss curriculum design, as well as observe each other in the classroom; teachers organising CPD sessions and teaching and learning conferences together, as well as professional dialogue and the dissemination of research findings and materials, and the sharing of good practice.

Effective communication with parents can be achieved by involving parents in a school's preparation for transition and by developing their understanding of the culture of the new school, helping them understand what to expect. In practice, this might include promoting and enhancing the role of parent/carer partnerships such as through the use parent/carer advisers as explained by Greenhough et al. in their 2007 paper and by the DCSF in 2008. It can also be achieved using parent voice mechanisms which gather, monitor and evaluate parental views in relation to transfers and transitions and give feedback and updates to parents showing how the school has listened to and responded to parents' questions and concerns.

Effective communication with pupils can be achieved by providing information about what to expect at each stage of the transfer process and where and who to go to for help or to have questions answered, as explained by Sanders et al (2005). It can also be achieved by ensuring that pupils are involved in the transition process at all stages, and are well informed of what to expect in their new school, as outlined by Schulting et al. (2005) and LoCasale-Crouch et al. (2008).

Feature 3 - School visits and induction programmes should be given priority

School visits and induction programmes can improve social and academic outcomes if they are given priority and invested in. In other words, to be effective, they need to be well-planned and appropriately resourced and staffed.

School visits work best when they are planned and publicised long before pupils transfer in order to give pupils and their parents/carers a good understanding of the new school and its systems and structures, expectations and routines. Induction programmes also work best when the teachers involved are provided with appropriate training and detailed information about what they're expected to achieve. The induction also needs to be well structured and engaging with high quality resources. The planning and teaching of induction programmes needs to involve the core subjects of English, maths and science. Ideally, prior to induction and as part of the school visits, pupils in primary schools should be enabled to make regular use of secondary school facilities in order to become familiar with secondary teachers, buildings and methods. Where daytime visits by primary pupils is not possible, after school clubs run by secondary teachers for pupils from their feeder primaries is a useful means of encouraging future pupils to become familiar with their new school prior to transfer.

Feature 4 - Differentiate the transition experience for all pupils

Different types of pupils experience the transfer and transition process in different ways. As such, they require different types of support and at different stages of the process. In practice, this might take the form of identifying vulnerable pupils and assigning a dedicated teaching assistant to them to provide additional guidance and skills development. It might mean modifying the process for pupils with special educational needs and disabilities (SEND), consulting educational psychologists, for example, about the emotional impact of life changes on vulnerable young people. It might mean establishing dedicated summer schools for those pupils who are identified as at risk of falling behind at the start of the new academic year and continuing to work with them to ensure the gap does not widen in the intervening weeks between the end of Year 6 and the beginning of Year 7. For more, see Taverner et al. (2001).

Feature 5 - Senior leaders need to support transition and all staff need clearly defined roles and responsibilities

A smooth and successful transition process depends on the whole school coming together, working effectively as one in the interests of pupils' social, emotional and academic success. To achieve this, all school staff need clearly defined roles and responsibilities, and senior staff need to provide effective leadership for transition which means being engaged in all aspects of the process.

In practice, this means that the headteacher and senior leadership team must provide their full support for the transition process - financially, in terms of resources, and psychologically. There needs to be a designated senior leader responsible for transition with the status to give it importance and able to align these processes with wider school improvement priorities.

This also means that all other school staff have clearly defined responsibilities for transition. For example, there will be a member of staff who is the school's named person responsible for meeting parents/carers who want to drop in and discuss issues. They will be another member of staff responsible for managing data on new pupils (including prior attainment at Key Stages 1 and 2, and teacher assessments). And there will be a member of staff responsible for listening and responding to pastoral issues amongst new pupils.

In terms of senior leaders 'putting their money where their mouths are' by allocating appropriate resources to enable a smooth and successful transition, this might mean timetabling experienced teachers in Year 7 and, where possible, making teaching assistants available to provide in-class support for the first half term immediately following transfer. TAs are particularly useful because they can contribute to assessment, support pupils with SEND, provide valuable insights into the needs of individual pupils and maintain established routines when they change classes with individual pupils.

Senior leaders can also play a vital role in ensuring that high quality data is available for every pupil joining a new school, and in establishing a clear strategic vision for strengthening transfers and transitions through the work of the governing body, self-evaluation and the school improvement plan. Senior leaders and other staff with responsibility for transition can aid the transition process by developing a transfer and transitions policy that aligns with the school improvement plan and contributes to raising standards and closing attainment gaps between identified groups. And, finally, they can engage with and contribute to local and national plans to share effective practice and develop consistency. Talking of sharing best practice...

Feature 6 - Share best practice

The transfer and transition process can be further improved if examples of good practice are identified and disseminated. For example, schools could engage with local and national research evidence about various aspects of transfer. Senior leaders, teachers and other adults who work with pupils and/or their families could engage in professional development activities including action research. And groups of schools could work together to build leadership capacity and develop a greater knowledge base by involving pupils and parents/carers in the monitoring, reviewing and planning process, and by strategically sharing effective practice.

APPENDIX
Transition to post-16

This book, like most literature about transition, focuses on pupils' experience of transfer from primary to secondary school, as well as between the various years and key stages of compulsory schooling. However, whilst working with FE colleges across the country, it has struck me how important the transition from school to FE is and just how unprepared students are for this change. By way of an appendix, therefore, I'd like to remedy the situation and offer some advice on how to improve the transition of older students from Key Stage 4 to further education, be that in the form of the school sixth form, a sixth form college, an FE college or another training provider...

A common mistake FE teachers make - particularly when planning assignments - is to assume that in the six weeks between leaving school and starting college, students have - somehow, somewhere - acquired an armoury of study skills and, perhaps by a process of osmosis, have become adept at working independently.

Study skills, however, are not innate; rather, they must be taught - a process which is about making the implicit explicit, the invisible visible.

Teaching study skills about breaking down broad tasks into their constituent parts, modelling each process, then providing opportunities for students to practice and refine them.

For example, if an assignment requires students to research information for an essay, we must explicitly teach them how to use multiple sources, how to skim and scan for key facts, and how to distinguish between fact and opinion and detect bias. We must then teach them how to use evidence to support an argument, including how to embed quotations, and how to write a bibliography citing their sources.

Before students write their essays, we must teach them how to craft a logical argument, using text markers such as 'Firstly', 'Secondly' and 'Thirdly'; 'However", 'Therefore', and 'In conclusion'.

If we expect students to work independently, perhaps drafting and re-drafting work based on feedback, and to do so outside of lessons and without our support, we must teach them how to manage and organise their time, how to revise (avoiding cramming by distributing and spacing practice, and interleaving topics), and how to self-assess then re-draft, referring to the success criteria.

If we expect students to engage in classroom debates, we must teach them active listening skills and turn-taking, as well as how to agree or disagree with someone else's contributions without it becoming personal. Although school pupils frequently engage in classroom discussions, group talk is particularly crucial in FE because, as Lave and Wenger (1991) point out, adults, unlike children, learn through communities of practice; they learn by engaging in 'legitimate peripheral participation', by striving to engage with others to enter into the membership of a chosen group.

If we expect students to adopt a growth mindset, willingly accepting and acting on feedback, taking risks and regarding mistakes as an integral part of the learning process, then we must teach and model resilience. Growth mindset behaviours are likely to be developed in school but resilience and reflection become increasingly important in FE because, as Draper (1998), and Smith and Pourchot (1998) found, whilst both children and adults learn through experience and test all new learning against their prior experiences, the life experiences and contexts that adults bring with them to the classroom - and therefore how they respond to setbacks and assimilate new information within the context of prior knowledge - are different to the experiences and contexts that tend to accompany school pupils. In short, adults carry with them more prior knowledge and experiences and this colours how they learn new information and what they do with this new information.

Brookfield (2000) proposes that adulthood consists of its own, unique developmental phase and that, therefore, an adult is fundamentally not the same as a child. He argues that there are four developmental areas in which most adults advance:

1. Dialectical thinking (the recognition that specific sites make a nonsense of generalised rules and theories);
2. Practical logic (the power to make decisions to ignore logical certainties when it's in your personal interests to do so);
3. Epistemic cognition (becoming self-consciously aware of your learning styles); and
4. Critical reflection (acting knowingly, which - Brookfield suggests - is different from the critical reflection younger people are capable of).

Explicitly teaching and modelling study skills, therefore, is one means of bridging the gap between school and college but we shouldn't just teach skills at the start of a student's first year immediately following their transition from school. Instead, we must teach skills on a sliding scale as students progress from one year to the next and from one level of qualification to the next. For example, although we might start by teaching students how to write a simple bibliography, as they progress towards level 3 and HE programmes, we need to move on to Harvard referencing.

A useful starting point when planning the teaching of skills is to map the skills students need and when they need them. This needs to be done for every programme and for every level of qualification, noting the difference between a skill required at level one and a similar skill - albeit more developed and complex - at levels two and three.

Next, we should carry out an audit of students' existing skills and identify any gaps. This will, in turn, inform us of where to start and on which skills we should spend most of our time.

Once we have a skills map, we need to decide how and by whom these skills will be taught. For example, will it be the teacher's responsibility to explicitly teach and model skills before students are required to use them, or will a personal tutor be responsible for delivering study skills tutorials in standalone sessions?

Once a skill has been taught for the first time, we need to decide if it needs to be re-taught again when it is needed next (and, if so, whether we need to completely re-teach it or just recap and practice).

There are other considerations to take when bridging the gap between school and FE. For example, we need to decide what additional support is needed for students who require more explicit skills instruction than others? We need to dude whether to set aside study rooms for students to use for independent study and homework, and how to staff this facility so that students can access appropriate support if it's absent at home.

In short, we need to remember that the transition from school to FE is separated by a mere six weeks and that students are not immediately ready for the adult world of independence and responsibility. Rather, we must enable them to slowly adjust to college life and we must explicitly teach the skills and aptitudes required of them rather than assume they grow innately.

Bibliography

Belenky, DM, Nokes-Malach, TJ (2012), Motivation and Transfer: The role of mastery-approach goals in preparation for future learning. Journal of the Learning Sciences, 21(3), pp 399-432

Bennet, S, Kalish, N (2006), The Case Against Homework: How homework is hurting our children and what we can do about it. Crown. New York.

Biggs, JB, Rihn, BA (1984), The Effects of Intervention on Deep and Surface Approaches to Learning. In Kirby, JR (ED), Cognitive Strategies and Educational Performance (pp 279-293). Academic Press. Orlando.

Centre for Excellence and Outcomes in Children and Young People's Services, (2010), Effective Classroom Strategies for Closing the Gap in Educational Achievement for Children and Young People Living in Poverty, Including White Working Class Boys.

DCSF (2008), What Makes a Successful Transition to Secondary School?

DCSF (2009), Improving Reading: A Handbook for Improving Reading in Key Stages 3 and 4

DCSF (2009), Improving Writing: A Handbook for KS3

DCSF (2009), Narrowing the Gaps: From data analysis to impact: the golden thread

DfE (2011), How do Pupils Progress in Key Stages 2 and 3?

DfE (2012), Encouraging Reading for Pleasure: What the research says on reading for pleasure

DfES (2004), Transition and Progression Within Key

Stage 3.

Education Standards Research Team (2012), Research Evidence on Reading on Pleasure

Galton, M (1999), The Impact of School Transitions and Transfer on Pupil Progress and Attainment. Cambridge for DfEE.

Galton, M (2002), Research for Teachers: Transfer from the Primary Classroom. (www.tla.ac.uk)

GSR (2011), Investigating the Drop in Attainment During the Transition Phase With a Particular Focus on Child Poverty. (www.dera.ioe.ac.uk)

Hattie, J (2009), Visible Learning. Routledge. London.

Hattie, J (2012), Visible Learning for Teachers. Routledge. London.

Keith, TZ (1982), Time Spent on Homework and High School Grades: A large sample path analysis. Journal of Educational Psychology, 74, pp 248-253.

Mannion, J, Mercer, N, (2016), Learning to Learn: Improving attainment, closing the gap at Key Stage 3. The Curriculum Journal, 27:2, pp 246-271.

Marzano, RJ, Pickering, DJ (2007), Special Topic: The case for and against homework. Educational Leadership, 64(6), pp 74-79.

McGee, Mizelle (2004), Transition to Secondary School: A literature review. (www.researchgate.net)

National College for Teaching and Leadership (2013), Closing the Gap: How system leaders and schools can work together

National College for School Leadership / Curee (2010),

Leadership for Closing the Gap.

National Literacy Trust (2012), Literacy: State of the Nation

National Literacy Trust (2014), Literacy Guide for Secondary Schools

National Numeracy (2013), Essentials of Numeracy. (www.nationalnumeracy.org.uk)

NFER (2006), Transition from Primary to Secondary School: Current arrangements and good practice in Wales. (www.nfer.ac.uk)

Ofsted (2002), Changing Schools: Effectiveness of transfer arrangements at age 11.

Ofsted (2009), English at a Crossroads

Ofsted (2011), Excellence in English

Ofsted (2011), Removing Barriers to English

Ofsted (2012), Moving English Forward

Ofsted (2013), Improving Literacy in Secondary Schools: A Shared Responsibility

Ofsted (2015), Key Stage 3: The wasted years?

Palinscar and Brown (1982), Recriprocal Teaching of Comprehension – Fostering and Comprehension – Monitoring Activities; Cognition and Instruction, I (2), pp 117-175

Palmer, S (2001), How to Teach Writing Across the Curriculum. Ages 8-14 (A Writer's Workshop) 2nd Edition. Routledge. London.

Paschal, RA, Weinstein, T, Walberg, HJ (1984), The

Effects of Homework on Learning: A quantitative synthesis. Journal of Educational Research, 78(2), pp97-104.

Perkins, DN, Saloman, G (2012, Knowledge to Go: A motivational and dispositional view of transfer. Educational Psychologist, 47(3), pp248-258).

Pintrich, P, de Groot, E (1990), Motivational and Self-Regulated Learning Components of Classroom Academic Performance. Journal of Educational Psychology, 82, pp 33-40.

Robinson, V, Hohepa, M, Lloyd, C, (2009), School Leadership and Student Outcomes: Identifying what works and why (BES). Ministry of Education. Wellington, NZ.

Schagen, S, Kerr, D (1999), Bridging the Gap? The national curriculum and progression from primary to secondary school. National Foundation for Educational Research for DfEE.

Slavin, RE, (2010), Cooperative Learning: What Makes Groupwork Work? In Dumont, H, Istance D, Benavides, F (Ed), The Nature of Learning: Using research to inspire practice (pp161 – 178). OECD. Paris.

Sutton Trust/EEF (2015), Toolkit of Strategies to Improve Learning: Summary for schools spending the Pupil Premium.

Timperley, H, Wilson, A, Barrar, H, Fung, I, (2007), Teacher Professional Learning and Development: Best Evidence Synthesis Iteration (BES). Ministry of Education. Wellington, NZ.

Vatterott, C (2010), Five Hallmarks of Good Homework. Educational Leadership, 68(1), pp10-15.

Free preview of
Teach: The Journey to Outstanding
and
Teach 2: Educated Risks

I'm often asked to send free copies of my books to charity auctions or to schools and colleges to act as prizes at staff training days.

When I ask colleagues which book they'd like me to send, they invariably reply: just send whichever is your favourite.

But choosing my favourite book is a bit like choosing my favourite child. Only harder.

When push comes to shove, though, I usually pop a copy of *Teach* in the post. *Teach*, and now its sequel *Teach 2*, are probably my favoured offspring because they say most of what I want to say about teaching and learning.

They were labours of love to write and, between them, the culmination of about three years' toil at the keyboard and many more at the whiteboard.

So if you've enjoyed this book and haven't yet experienced *Teach* or *Teach 2*, then I'd encourage you to do so and, by way of temptation, here's a little summary of what I cover in those two tomes...

TEACH

The Bayesian Method - we're better together

In *Teach* I began by recounting the story of the American submarine, the USS Scorpion, which was declared lost on 5 June 1968 and all its ninety-nine crewmen presumed dead. Although an immediate search was initiated, it was without success because, with a potential search area stretching out thousands of square miles, it was like finding a needle in a haystack. Accordingly, the USS Scorpion was struck from the Naval Vessel Register on 30 June.

Later that year, however, another search led by John Craven (no, not the one from *Newsround*; the Chief Scientist of the US Navy's Special Projects Division) employed rather different methods to try to find the vessel. Dr Craven polled a wide array of specialists in various fields for their thoughts of where the sub might be. Their guesses were then pooled into a single average guess. This method draws on the Bayesian theory that was first deployed during the search for a hydrogen bomb lost off the coast of Palomares, Spain, in January 1966. Not one of the experts' guesses was right but the average of all their guesses was surprisingly accurate and led the recovery team to within just 183 metres of the lost sub.

In *Teach* I said that I believed in the Bayesian method of improving teaching and learning...

In other words, I confessed that I did not possess a panacea, I did not have an elixir, a pill which once popped would proffer outstanding teaching and learning every time, and I didn't expect any of my readers to know the secret to outstanding teaching and learning either. However – like Craven's team of experts – together, I believed we would find all the answers. In short – and I wanted this to be the motto of my book – I said that, as a teaching profession, we were better together.

The Pareto Principle - keeping the main thing, the main thing

The Nineteenth Century philosopher William James famously said that "the art of being wise is knowing what to overlook" and in *Teach* I advocated we should do just that. In other words, we should focus on the most important aspects of teaching and learning – the real drivers of change - and take small but sustainable steps forward. We should not adopt a different focus each week, whereby one initiative erases all memory of the last. Nor should we employ a 'one size fits all' approach that assumes that all aspects of our schools and colleges share the same strengths and weaknesses. Instead, we should ensure a personalised, common sense approach to improvement planning.

In *Teach* I also explained that economists have an 80/20 rule which they call "the law of the vital few" which is also known as the Pareto Principle – named after the Italian economist Vilfredo Pareto who observed in 1906 that 80% of the land in Italy was owned by 20% of the population. Joseph Juran developed the principle by observing that 20% of the pea-pods in his garden contained 80% of the peas. From this, we get the popular belief that 80% of the effects come from 20% of the causes. In business, for example, it is believed that 80% of sales come from 20% of customers.

It follows, therefore, that to achieve great teaching and learning in our schools and colleges we should focus on improving the 20% of things that create the most value. We'll get stronger results if we spend our time practising the most important things and even if we already do the most important things well, there is real value in practising them further because the value of practice increases once the thing being practised has been mastered. In *Practice Perfect* Doug Lemov et al say that to keep practising something once we've already mastered it is to develop automaticity, fluidity, and creativity.

There's another advantage to focusing on the main thing. As Ben Levin – the former Deputy Director of Education in Ontario – says, "One of the challenges in education is that the pizzazz is around having the seemingly new idea, whereas the real work is in making it happen... Having a great new idea is less important to success than getting ordinary things done correctly and efficiently". The main thing has to be about what works in the classroom because, as Paul Black and Dylan Wiliam say in their book *Inside the Black Box*, "Standards are raised only by changes which are put into direct effect by teachers and students in classrooms".

The Big 3 - learning from the evidence

In deciding what the 'main thing' is, I believe in evidence-based practice. I believe we should use evidence gleaned from our own observations and from wide-ranging discussions with colleagues, as well as from quality external sources. In *Teach* I argued that there are three aspects of formative assessment in particular which I believe hold the key to unlocking the secret of great teaching. I called these three strategies the 'Big 3' and they were:

1. Pitch,
2. Questioning, and
3. Feedback.

These three strategies underpinned *Teach* because I was certain - and still am for that matter - that they are in the 20% of drivers, they are 'the main things' that if improved will lead to great teaching and learning.

The best of the rest - but no spoilers

In *Teach* I explored at length what the 'Big 3' - pitch, questioning and feedback - meant in practice. I also examined what 'outstanding' teaching and learning really looked and felt like. It's impossible to do justice to a 60,000-word book in this short introduction - and nor would I want to for the sake of my royalties! - but here is my best attempt at summarising the general tone and content of that book to aid your enjoyment and understanding of the text you now hold in your hands...

What is outstanding teaching and learning?

There is no silver bullet, no secret formula for teaching outstanding lessons – what works is what's best. The best thing to do, therefore, is to get to know your students by regularly assessing them and then to plan for progress by providing opportunities for all your students to fill gaps in their knowledge.

Learning is invisible and cannot be observed in a single lesson. A lesson does not exist in isolation; it is all about context, so it is better to think of a lesson as one learning episode in a long series. It does not necessarily need a neat beginning and end or to be in four parts and it does not need to prescribe to a particular style of teaching. For example, every lesson does not need to include opportunities for group work or independent study. A lesson can be meaningfully spent with students reading or writing in silence so long as, in the wider context of the series, there is a variety of learning activities.

The best teachers are sensitive to the needs of their students and adjust their lessons to the 'here and now'. Students work best for the teachers who respect them, know their subjects, and are approachable and enthusiastic. The most effective teachers are relentless in their pursuit of excellence and are able to explain complex concepts in a way which makes sense.

Outstanding teaching takes place when all students make progress over time. Students make progress over time when they are challenged and engaged. That is why the *Big 3* - the strategies I recommend you focus on in order to improve the quality of teaching - are: pitch (providing challenge); questioning (encouraging engagement); and feedback (leading to progress).

Learning takes place when certain cognitive principles are observed, including: factual knowledge must precede skill; memory is the residue of thought; we understand new concepts in the context of things we already know; it is impossible to be good at something without deliberate practice; and intelligence can be changed through hard work.

The 1st strategy in the Big 3: Pitch

Students are more likely to get better at something if they believe intelligence can be changed through hard work. The word 'yet' can be a powerful tool in the teacher's toolbox: "I can't do this... *yet.*"

The best classrooms are those in which students feel welcomed, valued, enthusiastic, engaged, eager to experiment and rewarded for hard work. The way to achieve this is to prize effort over attainment and focus on progress (learning) not outcomes.

If the work is too easy, students will switch off; if the work is too hard, students will switch off. Work must be pitched in the 'zone of proximal development' – hard but achievable with support. If something's too easy, we rely on our memory instead of thinking (e.g. $1 + 1 =$); if it's too hard, we run out of processing power (e.g. $46 \times 237 =$) and stop thinking; if it's challenging but achievable and we are successful, our brains reward us with a dose of dopamine which is pleasurable and binds neurones together creating memories. This is learning.

Desirable difficulties make information harder to encode (learn initially) but easier to retrieve later. This leads to deeper learning. We achieve desirable difficulties by:

spacing learning apart with increasingly long gaps; interleaving topics rather than finishing one topic then moving onto another; testing frequently – using low stakes quizzes at the start of topics/lessons to identify prior learning as well as knowledge gaps, and to interrupt forgetting; and making learning materials less clearly organised so that students have to think hard about the materials (e.g. using a difficult-to-read font).

At its simplest, learning is concerned with the interaction between our environment, our working memory and our long-term memory. Our working memory is about awareness and thinking; our long-term memory is about factual knowledge and procedural knowledge. We can improve the speed and ease with which we retrieve information from our long-term memory and transfer it into our working memory (where we can use it) by making connections between new and existing information – applying prior knowledge to new knowledge.

Prior knowledge helps us to 'chunk' information together, saving precious space in our limited working memory, allowing us to process more information. For example, the acronym 'BBC' takes one space in our working memory whereas, without the prior knowledge that the BBC is a TV company, the letters B, B and C would take three spaces. Prior knowledge is domain-specific. We know BBC whereas people in Japan would know WMBC. They'd take one space to remember WMBC whereas we would take four spaces to remember W, M, B and C.

When planning lessons, we should focus on what students will be made to think about rather than on what they will do. We might, for example, organise a lesson around a big question.

We need to repeat learning several times – at least three times, in fact – if it is to penetrate students' long-term memories.

Tests interrupt forgetting and reveal what has actually been learnt as well as what gaps exist. Accordingly, we should run pre-tests at the start of every unit – perhaps as a multiple choice quiz – which will provide cues and improve subsequent learning. Retrieval activities like this also help students prepare for exams.

Information 'sticks', so to speak, when each lesson clearly articulates and is built around a simple idea – i.e. when the teacher is clear about the key take-away message from each lesson, which could be a question or hypothesis.

Information also sticks when we use metaphor to relate new ideas to prior knowledge and to create images in students' minds.

Information sticks when we pique students' curiosity before we fill gaps in students' knowledge (thus convincing students they need the information). This can be done by asking students to make predictions or by setting a hypothesis to be proven or disproven.

Information sticks when we make abstract ideas concrete by grounding them in sensory reality (i.e. you make students feel something). The richer – sensorily and emotionally – new information is, the more strongly it is encoded in memory.

Information sticks when ideas are made credible by showing rather than telling students something (e.g. experiments, field studies, etc. beat textbooks for 'stickability').

The 2nd strategy in the Big 3: Questioning

Classroom discussion – best achieved through artful questioning – makes students smarter because it makes students think. Questions should only be used if they cause thinking and/or provide information for the teacher about what to do next (in other words, we should avoid the 'guess what's in my head' charade). The most common model of teacher talk is IRE: initiation, response, evaluation. But it doesn't work very well. A better model is ABC: agree/disagree with, build upon, and challenge whereby students pass questions around the classroom. The Japanese call this *neriage* which means 'to polish' – students polish each other's answers, refining them, challenging each other's thinking.

Increasing wait time – the amount of time the teacher waits for an answer to their question before either answering it themselves or asking someone else – makes students' answers longer, more confident, and increases students' ability to respond.

Good questions are an expressive demonstration of genuine curiosity, have an inner logic, are ordered so that thinking is clarified and are a part of an ongoing dialogue. In open questions, the rubric defines the rigour. In multiple-choice questions – which, as above, are effective ways of interrupting forgetting – the options define the rigour. Effective assessment combines open and multiple-choice questions.

The 3rd strategy in the Big 3: Feedback

Feedback is information given to students about their performance relative to their targets. Feedback should redirect the student's and the teacher's actions to help the student achieve their target. Effective feedback: addresses faulty interpretations; comments on rather than grades work; provides cues or prompts for further work; is timely, specific and clear; and focused on task and process rather than on praising.

Feedback works best when it is explicit about the marking criteria, offers suggestions for improvement, and is focused on how students can close the gap between their current and their desired performance; it does not focus on presentation or quantity of work.

Feedback can backfire – it needs to cause a cognitive rather than emotional reaction – i.e. it should cause thinking.

Feedback can promote the growth mindset if it: is as specific as possible; focuses on factors within students' control; focuses on factors which are dependent on effort not ability; and motivates rather than frustrates students.

Self- and peer-assessment can be effective strategies because they: give students greater responsibility for their learning; allow students to help and be helped by each other; encourage collaboration and reflection (useful skills for life); enable students to see their progress; and help students to see for themselves how to improve.

Improving student' ability to self- and peer-assess can help raise their levels of achievement but self- and peer-assessment needs to be used wisely. Students need to be helped to develop the necessary skills and knowledge because research suggests that 80% of the feedback students give is wrong.

The only useful feedback is that which is acted upon – it is crucial that the teacher knows the student and knows when and what kind of feedback to give, then plans time for students to act on feedback (e.g. DIRT - directed improvement and reflection time).

And that, in a nutshell, was what I said in *Teach*. So good they made a sequel.

TEACH 2

Teach 2 is a sequel of sorts but it's not essential you've read the first book because you won't find any exciting cliffhangers being resolved in the pages of that book, or unravel any twisted plot-lines within the well-worn folds of its dust-jacket.

Instead, *Teach 2* says some of the things I forgot to say in *Teach* as well as some of the things I've learnt since writing the first book.

And one of the things I've learnt since writing the first book is that motivation requires: A destination to aim for – knowing what the outcome looks like and not giving up until you reach it; a model to follow – an exemplar on which to base your technique; a coach – someone who is regarded as an expert and who sets high expectations; regular checkpoints to show what progress has been made and what's still to do; regular celebrations of ongoing achievements; messages about upcoming milestones – being encouraged to "up your game" when achievements are within your grasp; and a degree of personalisation – the ability to make choices about how to carry out tasks in order to increase enjoyment and engagement.

What makes a great teacher?

Like master coaches, the best teachers teach in chunks: they show students the end result then break it up into its constituent parts. They don't expect their students to make vast progress overnight, they look for gradual improvements and suggest minor tweaks, they encourage their students to take one day at a time, to draft and re-draft, to slowly and incrementally get better. Great teachers understand the importance of repetition, of doing something – practising a skill, drilling for knowledge – over and over again until it becomes automatic.

Great teachers possess a vast grid of task-specific knowledge that allows them to creatively and effectively respond to a student's efforts. They want to know about each student so they can customise their communications to fit the larger patterns in a student's life. They are able to deliver information to students in a series of short, vivid, highly focused bursts. They don't necessarily speak in a dictatorial tone but they do deliver their instructions in a way that sounds urgent and clinical. They have a moral honesty and use their character and personality to great effect.

Expert teachers have high levels of knowledge and an understanding of the subjects they teach. They combine the introduction of new subject knowledge with students' prior knowledge; they can relate current lesson content to other subjects in the curriculum; and they make lessons uniquely their own by changing, combining and adding to the lessons according to their students' needs and their own teaching goal. They are therefore able to predict and determine the types of errors that students might make, and this means that they can be much more responsive to students.

Great teachers are relentless in their pursuit of excellence and their language with students is infused with this sense of urgency and drive. They need not argue about expected standards of behaviour. They achieve this in different ways – sometimes through the gravitas of maturity and experience, sometimes through warm, interpersonal interactions with every student. They have the ability to explain complex concepts in ways that make sense, they ask good questions and give really good feedback – however it is done, students feel that they are learning, they know where they stand and feel confident about the process.

The best teachers aren't great just because they deliver information, they're great because they create lasting connections. They're not about the words they say, they're about the way they make students feel. In short, great teachers know and care about their students. In short, great teachers make personal connections with their students. Although pedagogical and content knowledge is important, great teachers know that what matters most is how they apply that knowledge.

We refer to it as "teaching practice" for a reason – we are forever practising, forever striving towards excellence and expertise. And yet we will never master it. But great teachers never tire of trying new things, of taking risks. They experiment and evaluate; they try and reflect.

What is great teaching?

Aristotle once said that "excellence is not an act but a habit", and so it is with teaching: the foundations of a successful classroom are built of rules and routines, regularly repeated and reinforced. With this in mind, it is important that you firmly and frankly set out your rules on day one, immediately establishing who's boss – because if you don't articulate clear dos and don'ts before you start teaching then you will find it difficult to break the bad habits that inevitably fill the void. For example:

1. You should always have a seating plan for every class you teach, adapted for every classroom you teach in. A seating plan serves two purposes: first, it helps you to learn the names of your students because seating them where you want gives you a useful reference point; second, it helps establish your authority in the room by dictating who sits with whom, forbidding the formation of friendship groups – and in so doing, it makes clear that your lesson is a place for learning not for socialising.

2. You should learn your students' names as quickly as you can and use their names as often as you can. Ask students if they have a preferred name or (clean, sensible) nickname. You will be surprised how powerful this can be in making them feel valued.

3. You should try to strike a positive balance whereby you reward good behaviour or effort three times more often than you sanction unacceptable performance. Where possible, signpost the right actions as a means of highlighting and correcting the wrong ones. When you need to sanction a student, make sure you hold firm. Always follow the school's behaviour policy and do not allow students to negotiate with you or argue about the unfairness of life. You should also strive to be consistent and fair in what misdemeanours you sanction students for.

4. You should establish clear routines for the beginnings and ends of lessons - you can make or break a lesson in the first few minutes. You need to establish your authority and show them that your classroom is your domain. Make students line-up outside – at least for the first lesson – and only enter once they are silent, attentive, and have removed their coats.

5. You should plan lessons backwards - rather than looking at a blank sheet of paper and thinking up fun activities to fill it, you should start your lesson planning at the end – with the objective. By formulating your objective first, you are forced to ask yourself "What will students understand today?" (which is measurable) rather than "What will students do today?" (which is not). A lesson activity can only be successful if it enables students to achieve the lesson's objective in a way that can be assessed – whether or not an activity is fun is of secondary importance if not entirely irrelevant.

What do high expectations look like?

The higher the expectations you have of somebody, the better they perform. It follows, therefore, that having high expectations of students is not only a nice thing to do, it actually leads to improved performance. Having high expectations is simply about establishing a set of clear rules and routines. For example, teachers who have high expectations often operate a "no opt out" policy. In other words, a teaching sequence that begins with a student unable to answer a question ends with the same student answering the question as often as possible.

Teachers who have high expectations always insist that "right is right" - they set and defend a high standard of correctness in their classroom. For example, they use simple positive language to express their appreciation of what a student has done and to express their expectation that he or she will now complete the task. They also insist that students answer the question they have asked not a different question entirely. These teachers are clear that the right answer to any question other than the one they have asked is, by definition, wrong. As well as insisting on the right answer, teachers with high expectations insist that students answer the right question at the right time. They protect the integrity of their lesson by not jumping ahead to engage an exciting right answer at the wrong time. These teachers insist their students use precise, technical vocabulary.

As well as having high expectations of our students, we should insist that our students have high expectations of themselves because only by believing in yourself and in your own ability to get better will you actually do so. This means students should have a growth mindset and believe that they can get better at anything if they work hard. They need to accept that work has to be drafted and redrafted, following the maxim that if it isn't excellent, it isn't finished. Students should also seek out and welcome feedback. They should value other people's opinions and advice and use it to help them improve their work. Feedback should be given and received with kindness in a manner that is helpful and not unduly critical, and yet it should be constructive and specific about what needs to be improved.

What are the habits of academic success?

I don't believe in conspiracy theories. I do, however, believe in coincidence. So what's the difference? When you think about it, coincidences are perfectly rational because they express a simple, logical pattern of cause and effect. Take, for example, academic achievement. Several years ago while working as a deputy headteacher I interviewed fifty students in years 11 and 13 who had achieved high grades in their GCSE and A level exams. I found something spooky – an apparent conspiracy.

For example, all the students I interviewed had an attendance of more than 93 per cent; 90 per cent of them had a perfect attendance record. All the students I interviewed told me they used their planners regularly and considered themselves to be well-organised. As a result, all the students I interviewed completed their homework on time and without fail. All the students I interviewed told me they always asked for help from their teachers when they got stuck. Most of the students I interviewed were involved in clubs, sports, or hobbies at lunchtime, after school and/or at weekends.

All the students believed that doing well in school would increase their chances of getting higher paid and more interesting jobs later in life. Many of them had a clear idea about the kind of job they wanted to do and knew what was needed in order to get it. They had researched the entry requirements and had then mapped out the necessary school, college, and/or university paths. They had connected what they were doing in school with achieving their future ambitions.

Was it spooky that nearly all these high-achieving students had done the same things? Or was it a simple case of cause and effect: because these students shared these traits they went on to succeed? I believe it was the latter: it was because these students had attended school, were well-organised, completed work on time, and had an end goal in mind that they had achieved excellent grades in their final exams.

The cause was diligent study and determination; the effect was high achievement. As such, these young people can teach our students a valuable lesson - the recipe for success is to: Have good attendance and punctuality; be organised and complete all work on time; be willing to ask for help when you're stuck; have something to aim for and be ambitious; map out your career path and be determined to succeed.

One means of becoming better organised is to acquire effective study skills and the following study skills are proven to be particularly helpful to students: *Self-quizzing* is about retrieving knowledge and skills from memory and is far more effective than simply re-reading a text. When your students read a text or study notes, you should teach them to pause periodically to ask themselves questions – without looking in the text. Once they have self-quizzed, get your students to check their answers and make sure they have an accurate understanding of what they know and what they don't know. You should space out your students' retrieval practice. This means studying information more than once and leaving increasingly large gaps between practice sessions.

Elaboration is the process of finding additional layers of meaning in new material. It involves relating new material to what students already know, explaining it to somebody else, or explaining how it relates to the wider world.

Generation is when students attempt to answer a question or solve a problem before being shown the answer or the solution. The act of filling in a missing word (the cloze test) results in better learning and a stronger memory of the text than simply reading the text.

Reflection involves taking a moment to review what has been learned. Students ask questions such as: What went well? What could have gone better? What other knowledge or experience does it remind me of? What strategies could I use next time to get better results?

Calibration is achieved when students adjust their judgment to reflect reality – in other words, they become certain that their sense of what they know and can do is accurate. We need to teach our students to remove the illusion of knowing and actually answer all the questions even if they think they know the answer and that it is too easy.

How can we close the gender gap?

There are five key "gaps" in the educational outcomes of boys and girls – reading skills, reading for pleasure, maths performance, STEM uptake, and STEM careers. First, boys lag behind girls at the end of compulsory education in reading skills by the equivalent, on average, of a year's schooling. Second, boys are far less likely to spend time reading for pleasure. Third, and in contrast, boys perform better than girls in maths, although the gender gap is narrower than in reading. Fourth, there remain significant disparities in the subjects boys and girls choose to study, with girls less likely to choose scientific and technological fields of study than boys.

Finally, even when girls choose these subjects they are less likely to take up careers in related fields. This widens the gap later in life in the career and earning prospects of women. Furthermore, boys in OECD countries are eight percentage points more likely than girls to report that school is a waste of time. Meanwhile, in higher education and beyond, young women are under-represented in maths, science, and computing. In 2012, only 14 per cent of young women who entered university for the first time chose science-related fields of study, including engineering, manufacturing and construction. By contrast, 39 per cent of young men who entered university that year chose to pursue one of those fields of study.

Some people believe that the attainment gap between boys and girls is the result of biological differences. After all, there are more than a hundred genetic differences between the male and female brain. For example, according to Blum (1997), boys' brains generally have more cortical areas dedicated to spatial-mechanical functioning, whereas girls' brains generally have greater cortical emphasis on verbal-emotive processing. As a result, girls tend to use more words than boys and girls tend to think more verbally. On the other hand, some people believe that the gender gap can be explained by differences in attitude not biology; aptitude, they argue, knows no gender. According to many international reports on the gender gap in education – most notably perhaps a 2012 OECD report called *Closing the Gap: Act Now* – boys and girls, men and women, when given equal opportunities, have an equal chance of achieving at the highest levels.

In the final analysis, it doesn't matter whether we believe the gender gaps in education are the result of biology or attitude – or indeed, as seems most likely to me, a nuanced combination of the two. What matters most is that we teachers believe that the gaps can and should be closed so here are some possible strategies for closing the gaps in literacy and STEM:

Closing the gap in literacy

1. Schools should promote reading for enjoyment and involve parents (particularly fathers) in their reading strategies. Schools should provide students with opportunities to read around their own interests, and enjoy reading. Schools should have a reading strategy and should focus on the needs of groups of students who are more likely to fall behind – including boys – as well as the effectiveness of the school library in supporting these strategies.

2. Every teacher should have an up-to-date knowledge of reading materials that will appeal to disengaged boys.

Schools should have a library at their heart and the school librarian should play an important role in enthusing teachers with the knowledge of reading materials. Schools should be encouraged to invest in their library provision.

3. School libraries should target students (particularly boys) who are least likely to be supported in their reading at home, perhaps by working in partnership with children's centres to target younger families who most need support. Libraries should also encourage students to take part in important initiatives, such as the annual Summer Reading Challenge initiative.

4. Every boy should have weekly support from a male reading role-model. One boy in five thinks reading is more for girls than boys. This reflects the fact that mothers are more likely than fathers to support their children's reading, that mothers are more likely to read in front of their children, and that the teacher who teaches a student to read is more likely to be a woman. Many boys will be supported in their reading by males within the home, but for those who aren't, the recruitment of male reading volunteers is a helpful strategy for schools to employ. Schools could make use of volunteering initiatives to engage young men in the support of boys' reading.

Closing the gap in STEM

1. Ensure students have a solid foundation in mathematics because evidence shows that studying maths for longer increases the average grade in biology and chemistry more than studying biology and chemistry.

2. Help students to develop their spatial skills because, although it is stereotypical to say that women have poor spatial awareness and a claim without scientific evidence of genetic or hormonal differences between the genders, spatial skills are malleable through practice and

improving spatial skills has proven, in the US, to improve the retention of engineering students.

3. Emphasise the importance of communication skills in the practice of science and engineering, thereby changing the perception that individuals cannot be gifted or skilled in both maths and languages. The vast majority of STEM jobs involve team-work, which necessitates communication. Despite the importance of communication to engineering, interpersonal communication and collaboration skills are generally portrayed as the opposite of maths and science skills, implying that people are almost always more skilled in one than the other. However, research provides compelling evidence that communication skills are essential in engineering, and suggests that integrating maths and communication skills in engineering would be of particular benefit to female students.

4. Help students develop resilience because female students may feel apprehensive about performing on a spatial skills task because they fear that performing poorly will confirm the existing negative stereotype. This so-called "stereotype threat" may actually cause girls to perform worse than they would otherwise do and therefore the danger lies in the self-fulfilling prophecy. However, a mindset shift – whereby girls are presented with experiential accounts of the origins of stereotypes – can have measurable positive consequences to combat this downward spiral. Several popular studies by Professor Carol Dweck have found that focusing on the power of practice rather than innate talent can be a key motivator for students and teaching the power of a growth mindset allows girls to perform better, even when they understand the stereotypes against them.

5. Give female students an active expert role whereby they answer questions, make comments, teach others and express their own voice through presentation because it will make them feel like they belong to the expert group. Since this feeling of belonging is what girls

often lack in STEM fields, active expert roles can help girls in particular to enhance their sense of belonging to their classmates and to the learning material.

6. Have a clear marking policy that ensures constructive feedback is given to help girls to properly gauge their success since a study by sociologist Shelley Correll found that girls need a better picture of where they stand in maths and science classes than do boys because otherwise they will use their biased self-assessment. The implications of these studies are that marks and test scores in maths and science must be better explained to students and feedback must be clearer and more constructive.

7. Re-evaluate the use of group work because, while group work has often been encouraged as an exercise to build team-work and communication skills, a study on interpersonal communication which focused on gender and engineers versus non-engineers found that "engineering males were more likely than other groups to draw negative conclusions about speakers who engaged in self-belittlement by admitting to difficulties or mistakes – particularly with technological issues". Also, Debbie Chachra, in an editorial entitled *The Perils of Teamwork*, argues that asking students in STEM classes to work in teams does not have the desired supportive effect. Since school students have various levels of experience, they tend to divide based on skill-sets and self-efficacy. As such, girls are often given less technical and more managerial tasks. This can perpetuate a vicious cycle, says Chachra, to make girls feel that they do not belong in the maths and science fields.

How do students learn?

Students come to the classroom with preconceptions about how the world works. If their initial understanding is not engaged, they may fail to grasp any new concepts or information that is taught, or they may remember them for the purposes of a test but then revert to their preconceptions when outside the classroom. In order to develop competence in an area of inquiry, students must have a deep foundation of factual knowledge, understand facts and ideas in the context of a conceptual framework, and organise knowledge in ways that facilitate retrieval and application. A meta-cognitive approach to instruction can help students learn to take greater control of their own learning by defining learning goals and monitoring their progress in achieving them.

In order to help students become experts, we need to draw out and work with the pre-existing understanding they bring with them. This means actively inquiring into students' thinking, and creating classroom tasks and conditions under which student thinking can be revealed. We also need to teach less subject matter but cover the content we do teach in greater depth, providing many examples in which the same concept is at work and by so doing proffer a firm foundation of factual knowledge. And we need to teach meta-cognitive skills in order to enhance student achievement and develop students' ability to learn independently.

One practical means of doing this is to use constructive alignment, a concept that derives from cognitive psychology and constructivist theory and recognises the importance of linking new material to experiences in the learner's memory, as well as extrapolating that material to possible future contexts – connecting the learning, showing the bigger picture. The teacher makes a deliberate alignment between the planned learning activities and the learning outcomes. This is a conscious effort to provide the learner with a clearly defined goal, a well-designed learning activity that is appropriate for the task, and well-designed assessment criteria for giving feedback to the learner once they've completed that task. In constructive alignment you start with the outcomes you want students to learn, and then align teaching and assessment to those outcomes.

Constructive alignment marries well with the SOLO taxonomy which stands for "structure of observed learning outcomes" and helps to map levels of understanding that can be built into intended learning outcomes and create assessment criteria or rubrics. It consists of five levels of understanding: 1. Pre-structural: a student hasn't understood the point and offers a simple – incorrect – response; 2. Uni-structural: a student's response only focuses on one relevant aspect; 3. Multi-structural: here, a student's response focuses on several relevant aspects but these are treated independently of each other; 4. Relational: here, the different aspects seen at the multi-structural level have become integrated to form a coherent whole; 5. Extended abstract: the integrated whole is now conceptualised at a higher level of abstraction. As students move up the five levels, their understanding grows from surface to deep to conceptual. The SOLO taxonomy also helps develop a growth mindset because students come to understand that declarative and functioning learning outcomes are the result of effort and the use of effective strategies rather than the result of innate ability.

How can we teach students to transfer their learning?

The ability to extend what has been learned in one context to new contexts is called 'transfer' and helping our students to develop this skill is vital if we want them to be able to transfer what we teach them in one lesson to another lesson on a similar topic but this ability to transfer is not necessarily automatic; rather, we need to teach it. Several critical features of learning can affect a student's ability to transfer what they have learned. To help students to develop 'transfer' we should: allow a sufficient amount of time for initial learning to take place; plan for distributed – or spaced – learning and engage in deliberate practice; make sure students are motivated to learn by planning work with sufficient challenge; teach information in multiple, contrasting contexts and/or in abstract form; teach metacognition so that students become expert at monitoring and regulating their learning.

Why do students crave variety?

Students are more likely to want to learn - and to *actually* learn - if their interest is piqued by newness, by the extraordinary, by the unfamiliar. Students crave variety; they need lessons to surprise them, to excite them, to ignite new sparks and pose new questions. They need lessons to unsettle them, too; to discomfort and challenge them, not bore them with a Groundhog Day feeling of de ja vu all over again. In short, we all grow tired of repetition, of the predictable and prosaic, of the monotonous and mundane, and we all need a frequent frisson of freshness in our lives. But surely not all lessons can provide novelty value? Well, no, but in order to make ideas 'stick' we need to make them tangible because students find it hard to care about or understand abstract concepts. If we ground an abstract concept in sensory reality and thus engage our students' emotions, our students are made to care about something, they are made to feel something and this is an important part of the learning process because when we are exposed to new information, we process it then attempt to connect it to existing information (in other words, we try to assimilate new knowledge with prior knowledge). The richer – sensorily and emotionally – the new information is, and the deeper the existing information is engrained, the stronger we will encode the new information in our long-term memories.

Ensuring our lessons provide variety and novelty, therefore, helps to appeal to students' senses *and* engage their emotions - if nothing else, simply by piquing their interest in something out of the ordinary, we're waking them up, shaking them up and making them think - and therefore the information we teach them is more likely to be retained over the long-term. So try something new. Bring learning to life with something exciting, something different, something surprising. Be assured, however, that providing variety and novelty in this way - that teaching lessons which students will never forget - doesn't mean your lessons can't follow a regular, familiar structure - my plea relates *only* to your teaching methods *not* your lesson structure. In other words, in order to engage students and make lessons memorable, I'm suggesting you aim to use varied and novel teaching approaches and strategies (activities or tasks, if you like) but that you continue to organise the learning in a logical - perhaps even predictable - way. So...

What's the secret of great lesson planning?

You can't prescribe the unpredictable; you can't dictate differentness but you can derive a set of fundamental rules or guidelines for what constitutes an effectively *planned* and organised lesson because even unique lessons which are full of surprise possess some common elements of design and obey a set of shared principles - what we might call our 'design for learning' or our 'five point plan':

Firstly, well-planned lessons **connect the learning** in three ways: 1. They articulate a clear learning goal that students understand - in other words, students are told where the lesson is headed. 2. They articulate a clear purpose for the learning - in other words, students are told why the learning goal is important and why they are learning what they're learning. 3. They ensure that students' starting points (what they already know as well as their misconceptions) are identified through pre-tests.

Secondly, well-planned lessons **personalise the learning**. They ensure that the learning is tailored to meet individual needs and to match individual skills, interests, and styles. They also ensure that this diagnostic data about students' starting points and misconceptions (both that gathered from pre-tests and that gleaned from ongoing assessments) is used to inform the lesson planning process.

Thirdly, well-planned lessons **grab students' attentions**. They ensure that the learning activities get and maintain students' attentions from the very beginning by using sensory 'hooks' and by ensuring that the learning is appropriately paced, and appropriately varied and challenging.

Fourthly, well-planned lessons **teach less and learn more**. They ensure that students acquire the necessary experiences, knowledge and skills to meet the learning goals but in so doing they remember that less is more: they cover a smaller amount of curriculum content so that they can explore it in greater depth and detail - and from a range of different perspectives - than they would be able to achieve if they attempted to 'get through' more content.

Finally, well-planned lessons **make time for students to reflect**. They provide students with regular opportunities to reflect on their progress, to revise their thinking and to re-draft their work, acting on the formative feedback they receive from teacher-, peer- and self-assessments.

What motivates students?

The first step towards encouraging students to produce high-quality work is to set assessment tasks which inspire and challenge them and which are predicated on the idea that every student will succeed, not just finish the task but produce work which represents personal excellence. The most effective assessment tasks offer students an opportunity to engage in genuine research not just research invented for the classroom. A student's finished product needs a real audience and the role of the teacher is to help students to get their work ready for the public eye. This means there is a genuine reason to do the work well, not just because the teacher wants it that way. Not every piece of work can be of genuine importance but every piece of work can be displayed, presented, appreciated, and judged.

Assessment tasks work best when they are structured in such a way as to make it difficult for students to fall too far behind or fail. Tasks also work best when they are broken into a set of clear components so that students have to progress through checkpoints to ensure they are keeping up. Good tasks have in-built flexibility to allow for a range of abilities. Assessment tasks work best when they have in-built rubrics which make clear what is expected of each student at each stage of development. In other words, the rubric spells out exactly what components are required in the assignment, what the timeline for completion is, and on what qualities and dimensions the work will be judged.

The best way of delivering all of the above is project-based learning which can also help students to become more creative, more positive and more independent. It helps if project-based learning forms part of the whole school culture, if it is common practice across all classes and year groups, and if it is the accepted mode of learning. There are three strands of project-based learning well worth remembering - indeed, in many ways, these three are the cornerstones of effective projects:

1. A genuine outcome - if students are to commit time and effort to their project, they need to know that there is a real audience and means of exhibition for their work. In other words, if students know their work is going to be put on public display, there to be critiqued by members of the public, including their family and friends and not just their teachers, they are more likely to work hard and produce their best quality work.

2. Multiple drafts - in real life, when the quality of work matters, we rarely submit our first attempt at something but in many schools students hand in their first attempt at something, have it marked and returned, then discard it before moving on to the next task. Project-based learning enables students to positively engage with the drafting and redrafting process, and encourages them to make time for and recognise the importance of polishing work until such a time as it represents their very best efforts. Producing multiple drafts is not only a great way of teaching students about the real life importance of redrafting, but it also provides great opportunities for personalised assessment.

3. Ongoing assessment - producing multiple drafts helps students to engage in formative assessment, learning from feedback and making gradual improvements. Re-drafting also enables students to learn from each other by critiquing each other's work. Regarded in this way, critique, - far from being a distraction or added burden - becomes integral to the learning process. Critique can become a lesson in its own right, providing opportunities for the teacher to give instruction, to introduce or refine concepts and skills. Such lessons can also bring students' misunderstandings to the fore, enabling the class to respond en masse.

Project-based learning also works best when students regard the project as personally meaningful and when it fulfils an educational purpose - in other words, when it is an integral part of the curriculum. A project can be made personally meaningful if teachers begin by triggering students' curiosity. In other words, at the start of the first lesson on the project, the teacher uses a 'hook' to engage students' interest and initiate questioning. A project can also be made personally meaningful to students if the teacher poses a big question which captures the heart of the project in clear, compelling language, and which gives students a sense of purpose and challenge. A project can be made personally meaningful to students if students are given some choice about how to conduct the project and present their findings. Indeed, the more choice, the better.

A project can fulfil an educational purpose if it provides opportunities to build metacognition and character skills such as collaboration, communication, and critical thinking, which will serve students well in the workplace as in life. A project can also fulfil an educational purpose if students conduct a real-life inquiry, rather than finding information in textbooks or on the Internet then making a poster. A project can also fulfil an educational purpose if it makes learning meaningful by emphasising the need to create high-quality products and performances through the formal use of feedback and drafting. A project can fulfil an educational purpose if it ends with a product being presented to a real audience. Work is more meaningful when it is produced not only for the teacher or the test but for a real public audience. This makes students care more about the quality of their work.

What is 'vision' and why does it matter?

A vision makes explicit what an organisation stands for and what its people want it to achieve; it binds people (staff, students, governors, the community, employers, and so on) together in the pursuit of a common goal and reminds them why they do what they do every day. A vision provides a focus for decision-making and conveys a picture of what the future will look like. An effective vision is desirable in that it appeals to long-term interests. It is feasible in that it comprises realistic, attainable goals and is focused in that it is clear enough to provide guidance in decision making. An effective vision is also flexible in that it is general enough to allow individual initiative and alternative responses in light of changing conditions. It is also communicable. In other words, it is easy to communicate and can be successfully explained within five minutes.

The vision needs to frame every conversation and speech, needs to focus every meeting, and inform every decision. It needs to be used like a mantra. It will remind people of their ultimate goal and refocus them on what's most important; it will convince them that they are playing a crucial role in helping to make the organisation's vision a reality and reassure them that they are helping to shape the future.

Is teaching a profession?

One such vision statement I worked with recently had at its heart the simple words "to ensure every student is challenged, engaged and making progress every day" because I wanted to strip away the sometimes distracting detail and focus on what fundamentally matters most in teaching - and if we cannot say that every student is challenged (i.e. doing something difficult), engaged (i.e. actively involved in the learning process and thinking for themselves), and making progress (i.e. learning something new each lesson and making progress over time) then we must surely have failed in our duty as educators.

For me, the most important words in that particular vision statement were 'all' and 'every day' because I firmly believed that it was not acceptable if some of our students were challenged but others were stuck or bored, it was not acceptable if some of our students were engaged but others were switched off or distracted, and it was not acceptable if some of our students were making progress but others were not learning anything at all. Equally, it was not acceptable if the lessons that were observed (be that formally or through learning walks, peer observations or coaching) were 'good' or 'outstanding' because they were an artificial showcase of what we could do when we tried really hard but what our students actually experienced on a normal day – and therefore what they experienced day in, day out, most of the time - was less than 'good'.

As such, that vision was really about achieving consistency and so at the beginning of that particular journey I had to wrestle with two apparently contradictory beliefs. On the one hand, I believed that teaching was a profession (as opposed to a job) and that teachers were professionals (as opposed to workers). It followed, therefore, that teachers should be afforded autonomy in the classroom rather than be dictated to by senior leaders. On the other hand, I believed that – in order to raise students' aspirations and improve outcomes – sometimes, senior leaders needed to balance their defence of teacher autonomy with their need to achieve school-wide consistency; sometimes, leaders needed to insist upon every teacher following a set of common working practices so that they could be sure that every student was in receipt of the same high standards of teaching because a child's birth should not be her destiny.

I ended my infernal internal debate by concluding that the level of autonomy afforded to teachers was dependent (to some extent, and notwithstanding their own professional experience and expertise) on where their school was along the path to excellence – schools needed to *tighten up* the constraints on autonomy in order to be 'good' but could *loosen* those constraints in order to become 'outstanding'. I also decided that we needed greater clarity around what, when schools did indeed loosen the constraints on autonomy, it really meant to be an autonomous teacher. Specifically, I decided we needed to stop thinking of autonomy in terms of individual, idiosyncratic habits of working alone and start thinking of autonomy in terms of collective autonomy, the kind of autonomy afforded to professionals in medicine and law and aviation.

Individual autonomy and professionalism were not, I decided, synonymous. Indeed, to be a professional was to work *as part of* a profession not to work idiosyncratically and in isolation. But perhaps collective autonomy and professionalism could become synonymous. Perhaps we could conflate the two terms and begin talking in terms of *professional autonomy* - and professional autonomy was about working with colleagues in a way that led to greater consistency and coherence, in a way that led to the same high standards of education being afforded to every student no matter their individual context. Professional autonomy was about supporting and challenging one another to ensure we all improved by reflecting on feedback, by analysing our impact, by engaging in deliberate practice and by learning from our mistakes just as we expected our students to do. And professional autonomy was also about working collectively to build the solid foundations of teaching, groundworks constructed of rules and routines regularly repeated and reinforced so that they come to be regarded as the 'standard operation' in every classroom in every corridor of the school.

Should teachers take risks?

Great teaching is about passing on established wisdom - to quote Matthew Arnold, "the best which has been thought and said". But it is about much more than this. It also establishes new meanings and forges new connections and understandings, it changes the self and the world around the self. Education is a social art - it is more than mere production or reproduction and if we view education in these terms then we must move beyond compliance and encourage greater risk-taking and greater experimentation in education. Education cannot conform, it cannot inflexibly follow a prescription if it is to focus on how we help our students to engage with, and thus come into, the world.

Teaching must have meaning beyond the facilitation of learning. In other words, teaching must have a meaning that comes from the outside and brings something radically new - it emancipates students. Students learn from the practices in which they take part, they learn by participating in a shared experience. It is only through the act of learning and engaging in classroom activity that they discover the meaning of the world; meaning cannot be derived without this interaction.

So if we are to regard education as a means of creating new knowledge and not just of 'passing on' existing knowledge then we must move beyond notions of compliance and conformity and encourage greater risk-taking and experimentation in the classroom. Teachers cannot inflexibly follow a lesson plan if they are to focus on helping students to engage with, and thus come into the world. And the purpose of education is, if nothing else, to help our students find their own way into the world and to create their own new beginnings, to forge their own futures.

It is, if you like, the ultimate pedagogical oxymoron: risk-taking within a set of rules and routines; freedom within a framework; autonomy within a profession. Or, to put it another way, it is an educated risk.

Is neuroscience the next cargo cult in education?

There's a now famous story about the residents of an island in the South Pacific who, during the Second World War, saw heavy activity by US planes bringing in goods and supplies for soldiers. For most islanders, this was the first time they'd seen this kind of technology. When the war ended, naturally so did the cargo shipments. Confused and keen to see the activity resume, some islanders built fake air-strips with wooden control towers, bamboo radio antennae, and fire torches instead of landing-lights. They believed this would attract more US planes carrying precious cargo. The physicist Richard Feynman used this event to coin the phrase "cargo-cult science". Just as the islanders' air-strips had the appearance of the real thing but were not functional, cargo-cult science refers to something that has the appearance of science but is actually missing vital elements of it. People involved in cargo-cult science use scientific terms and may even carry out research. But their thinking and – more crucially – their conclusions are scientifically flawed.

Neuroscience, it seems to me, is in danger of becoming the next cargo-cult. Although it sounds good, many references to the brain in educational books and articles are devoid of any real value and are what has come to be called "neurosophisms": the sophisticated but mistaken application of language associated with neuroscience. Neuroscience has certainly gained traction in recent years and people have become more interested in learning about how the brain works. This is, of course, a good thing and we should always encourage intellectual curiosity of this kind. It is partly what makes teaching a profession, after all.

The brain is fascinating and, although there remains much mystery about how it works, a lot more is now known that could influence the way we behave and, crucially, the way we teach and learn. However, if we insist on using neuroscience to explain common sense approaches to teaching, we are in danger of losing the debate by detracting from the real argument, by making the argument difficult to follow, or by making false connections between behavioural and physical phenomena.

Therefore, I would encourage you to question teaching advice that's presented as neuroscience and to be wary of salesmen who want your school to sign up to a programme backed by research from the field of cognitive neuroscience, especially if it comes adorned with pretty brain scans.

You can make a quick start simply by asking the following questions whenever you come across an article, book or marketing flyer that cites neuroscience: 1. Can I replace the word "brain" with the word "student" (or similar) without losing any of the meaning? 2. Is the advice being presented new or is it the product of common sense and experience and something I have been doing successfully in my classroom for years? 3. Is the research that is cited in support of the argument, psychological, educational or behavioural? If so, there is no need to defer to neuroscience.

About the author

M J Bromley is an experienced education leader, teacher, writer, consultant, speaker and trainer.

You can find out more about him and read his free blog at
www.bromleyeducation.co.uk

@mj_bromley

@mjbromley

/mjbromleytl

/mattbromleytl

Also by the author

BOOKS

Leadership for Learning
Ofsted: Thriving Not Surviving
A Teacher's Guide to Outstanding Lessons
A Teacher's Guide to Assessment
A Teacher's Guide to Behaviour Management
The Art of Public Speaking
How to Become a School Leader
Teach
School of Thoughts (ebook)
Teach 2: Educated Risks
The New Teacher Survival Kit

As Editor
SPaG Book (by Matilda Rose)
Outstanding Literacy (by Matilda Rose)

A member of the AUTUS GROUP LIMITED

Supporting schools and colleges in the UK

Consultancy
Critical friend service
Training and development
Open courses and in-house CPD
Copy-writing and marketing
Coaching and mentoring
Keynote speakers
School improvement
Self-evaluation
Policies and procedures
Inspection preparation
Teaching and learning

For more:

Follow Autus on Twitter.com/@AutusEd
Like Autus on Facebook.com/AutusEducation

AUTUS BOOKS
England, UK
Twitter: @AutusBooks

Making KS3 Count First Published 2016

Second Edition First Published 2017
Copyright © Bromley Education 2017

ISBN-13: 978-1975946883

ISBN-10: 197594688X

Printed in Great Britain
by Amazon